Moccasin flower (also known as lady's-slipper),
Minnesota's state flower. Postcard, ca. 1915.

MINNESOTA
Hail to Thee!

Built in 1902, Landmark Center in downtown St. Paul originally served as the Federal Court House and Post Office for the Upper Midwest. Destined for the wrecking ball in the 1970s, it was rescued and restored to its former grandeur by a group of dedicated citizens. Now on the National Register of Historic Places, this splendid castle-like building houses some of the capital city's premier cultural and arts organizations.

A SESQUICENTENNIAL HISTORY

MINNESOTA

Hail to Thee!

Karal Ann Marling

FOREWORD BY DON SHELBY

afton press

The publication of

MINNESOTA, HAIL TO THEE!
A Sesquicentennial History

and its distribution
to selected
Minnesota schools
has been
made possible by a
major gift from

TARGET

with additional
generous gifts from

Fred C. and Katherine B.
Andersen Foundation

Katherine B. Andersen Fund

Bailey Nurseries Foundation

Boss Foundation

Harlan Boss Foundation for the Arts

Home Federal Savings Bank

Laura Jane Musser Fund

Margaret Rivers Fund

The 2008 Minnesota
Sesquicentennial Commission

Frank W. Veden Charitable Trust

and

William and Bonnie Frels

Howard and Betsy Guthmann

Lowell and Cay Shea Hellervik

Thomas A. Keller III

John and Judy Kinkead

Bruce A. Larson

William J. and Pamela A. Lowe

George and Dusty Mairs

Malcolm and Patricia McDonald

Dick and Nancy Nicholson

Front cover: *Playing Kickball* (Lanesboro, Minnesota). Oil on canvas by Paul S. Kramer, 1983. Courtesy Minneapolis Club. Photo by Chuck Johnston.

Back cover: Guthrie Theatre. Photo by Jim Gallop, Gallop Studios, Minneapolis, Minnesota.

Edited by Michele Hodgson
Copyediting by Ashley Shelby
Designed by Mary Susan Oleson
Production assistance by Beth Williams
Printed by Pettit Network Inc., Afton, Minnesota

Library of Congress Cataloging-in-Publication Data

Marling, Karal Ann.
Minnesota, hail to thee! : a sesquicentennial history /
by Karal Ann Marling.—1st ed.
    p. cm.
Includes bibliographical references.
ISBN 978-1-890434-78-6 (hardcover : alk. paper)
1. Minnesota—History—Juvenile literature. I. Title.

F606.3.M37 2008
977.6--dc22

2007031933

Printed in China

Paul A. Verret
PRESIDENT

Patricia Condon McDonald
PUBLISHER

AFTON HISTORICAL SOCIETY PRESS
P.O. Box 100, Afton, MN 55001
800-436-8443
aftonpress@aftonpress.com
www.aftonpress.com

CONTENTS

acknowledgments   9
foreword   10
introduction   13

chapter one
BIRTHPLACE OF AMERICA?   25

chapter two
THE FORT, THE FALLS, THE RIVER   37

chapter three
FROM TERRITORY TO STATEHOOD   51

chapter four
A TALE OF TWO WARS   65

chapter five
WHEAT, TIMBER, FLOUR, IRON   83

chapter six
CELEBRATING, COMPETING, DEFINING   99

chapter seven
A THING OF BEAUTY   113

chapter eight
MODERN MINNESOTA   131

chapter nine
WHAT'S NEXT FOR MINNESOTA?   147

activities   152
bibliography   158
illustration credits   160
index   162

Present-day Fort Snelling, with the Mendota Bridge spanning the Minnesota River on the left. Oil painting by Paul S. Kramer, 1992.

ACKNOWLEDGMENTS

MY DEBTS TO MY FELLOW Minnesotans are enormous, especially to the kind listeners who called and wrote when I was working as a commentator for Minnesota Public Radio (with Chris Roberts) and KNOW 91.1 (with Steve Benson).

The generous staff members at the Minnesota Historical Society have provided hints, suggestions, documents, and prodding. They include Marcia Anderson, Debbie Miller, Kate Roberts, and Bonnie Wilson. The MHS also organized a forum for writers of sesquicentennial history at which its own historians were extremely helpful in their critique of this manuscript.

Patricia McDonald, Chuck Johnston, and Beth Williams of the Afton Historical Society Press have been kind and supportive throughout, as has editor Michele Hodgson. Mary Sue Oleson designed this book with care.

My friend Marilyn McGriff, former Isanti County historian and present-day historian of all things Minnesotan, deserves thanks for putting up with my discussions of obscure details of the runestone controversy and similar issues.

My friend and student Leigh Roethke* has inspired me by her own imaginative analyses of Minnesota history.

Seed portrait by Lillian Colton of author Karal Ann Marling.

*Leigh Roethke's Afton Press books for young readers include MINNESOTA'S CAPITOL: A Centennial Story and LATINO MINNESOTA.

FOREWORD

IN THE PAST THIRTY YEARS or so, history has lost its luster, its cultural importance—we've lost the notion that knowing one's history is as elemental as knowing one's name. I wish there were a single culprit or some grand conspiracy responsible for this loss, but it isn't quite that simple. As best as I can tell, the desire to teach and to learn our common sense of ourselves and the story of this place, our home, has been dampened by school boards and other well-meaning people who believe the school day isn't long enough to devote the same amount of attention to history *and* science, to history *and* math.

But it's not just that. I'm also told by this new breed of educator the world has changed. We don't share a common history anymore, they argue. Minnesota is no longer that Little Scandinavia with overlapping populations of Norwegians, Swedes, and Finns; instead, it is now home to the largest concentration of Hmong in one place outside of Laos. The state reports that more Somalis live here than in any other American city outside of New York. There are more Latinos and Russians and African-Americans here than ever before. They tell me: *See? Everybody here comes from some place else, dragging his or her own history behind.* What they seem to be saying is that there is nothing we can share with these newcomers.

Well, here's the thing: not much has, in fact, changed. The history of Minnesota is a history of newcomers. It is a history begun by people we only know as the Laurel, or the Mississippians, and later by the Dakota and Ojibwe—the original people. Then the state was staked and claimed by people from Scandinavia, Germany, Italy, Serbia, Croatia, Ireland, Africa, France, England . . . get an atlas. Each of these newcomers brought his or her own history to this new home and then created a new history here, one folded into the story of the state of Minnesota. It is this collective history that we ought to be studying, and sharing.

Karal Ann Marling has done us all a favor by giving us a celebratory history with, as the old folks used to say, "the bark on." We will, in this book, read of our greatest successes as well as our most shameful moments. And we will participate in the reading of this history with that peculiarly Minnesotan tendency, one that crosses all economic and class lines and pushes beyond boundaries of geography: our tendency to use the first person plural. We say "we" referring to our fellow citizens of today, and we say "we" when referring to the people who called this land home before settlers arrived. We say "we" when speaking of the people who broke this land, dreamed the western course of rail, trapped the beaver, fought one another, built the cities and churches a hundred and fifty years ago. "We" are Minnesotans.

When you read here of some grand accomplishment or contribution by a long-gone and, too often, forgotten Minnesotan, you will say: "We *did* that?" And you will be proud of yourself for no apparent reason, except for the fact that you are part of our history, too. You will also read here of the terrible things in our history, the things we would rather forget, but would only do so at our peril. And upon reading about these events, you will form the same words in silence: "We did *that*?"

I meet a lot of people who are coming to live in Minnesota for the first time. Prior to their arrival, many of them had no firsthand knowledge of its existence. They are armed with vague trivia: something about the Vikings or Twins, Scotch tape or a zillion lakes. In time they stub their toes on some Minnesota history and learn we were, and are, the first to volunteer in war and charity. They find out that a lot of those national politicians they had heard of came from here. Then one day, in a conversation with a relative back home in Toledo or Austin or Mogadishu or Vientiane, the newly minted Minnesotan will let slip the first person plural. Whenever I chance to overhear this, it never fails to give me a thrill.

In *MINNESOTA, HAIL TO THEE! A Sesquicentennial History,* Karal Ann Marling and the Afton Historical Society Press have given us a wonderful birthday present—our own story. Read it and share it, because it is a fairly certain bet that knowing where we've been is the surest way to know which way to go.

Now, write or call someone and say,
"We are 150 years old."
All of us.

Don Shelby
WCCO-TV and Radio

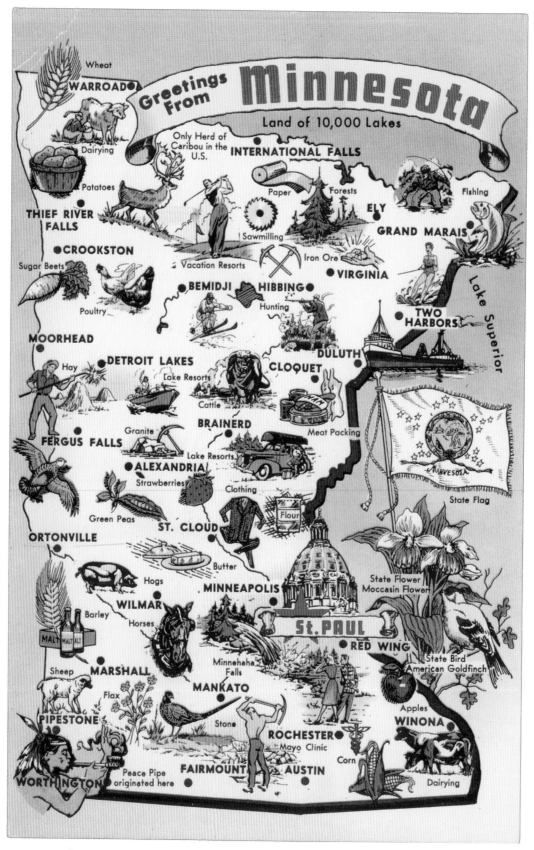

A 1960s postcard shows Minnesota's industries, products, and attractions.
Collectively, what do these symbols say about Minnesota?

INTRODUCTION TO THE NORTH STAR STATE

MINNESOTA IS THE NATION'S thirty-second state, admitted to the Union on May 11, 1858, just after California, the "Golden State" (1850), and just before Oregon, the "Beaver State" (1859). Minnesota is known as the "Land of 10,000 Lakes," although the latest count lists 11,842 of them. That's 3.3 million acres of fresh water!

Land of Many Names

Minnesota got its formal name from the Native Americans who lived in the forests, on the plains, and along the banks of the Mississippi River, long before explorers arrived from Europe. In the language of the Dakota Indians, Minnesota means "sky-tinted waters," a poetic way of describing all those beautiful lakes.

Sometimes called the "Gopher State," Minnesota is also known as the "the North Star State," which is a rough translation of the French phrase "*L'étoile du Nord*" (pronounced "lay twall doo nord"). This phrase appears on the state seal, a kind of Minnesota trademark that was suggested by Henry Sibley, the first governor of the state of Minnesota, and adopted by the legislature in 1861. The new state seal pictured a Native American on horseback being forced into the sunset by a pioneer with an ax, a rifle, and a plow. This seal described a sad fact of the 1860s: that adventurers, traders, and soldiers from Europe and Canada drove Minnesota's Native Americans from their traditional homelands. The motto of "L'étoile du Nord" was added to pay tribute to the French voyageurs, the hardy canoemen from Quebec who first explored Minnesota's natural resources. Like the voyageurs, Sibley had been a fur trader, and he was proud of their place in early state history.

Sibley's political enemies mocked him for putting on airs by selecting words for the state seal in Canadian French *patois* (slang), the only French he knew. Later observers have criticized his use of a picture drawn by frontier army officer Captain Seth Eastman because it seemed to approve of the forced removal of Indians from the lands that westward-pushing pioneers wanted to occupy. Captain Eastman's wife, Mary, who studied the Dakota culture, even wrote a poem about the meaning of the image in just those terms. "Give way, young warrior," her verse urged. Leave the Minnesota prairies: "The white man claims them now, / The symbols of his course are here, / The rifle, ax, and plough."

It was only during the civil rights era of the 1960s that Minnesotans objected to Sibley's seal. The fleeing Indian was replaced briefly by a white rider. In 1983, to put an end to the controversy, the Indian was returned to the official state seal. This time, however, he faced the settler squarely as his equal, riding southward into Minnesota on land they both shared.

State Symbols

Minnesota is rich in other official and semiofficial symbols. The state grain is wild rice, called *manomin* in the Ojibwe language. The state fish is the walleye, the state mushroom is the morel, and the state drink is milk. The state bird is the common loon, the state butterfly is the monarch, and the state gemstone is the Lake Superior agate. The state flower—the pink and white lady's-slipper—was chosen by the women who decorated the Minnesota displays at the World's Fair in Chicago in 1893. It took almost thirty more years for the legislature to approve their choice.

The present design of the Great Seal of the State of Minnesota became official in 1983. It depicts a barefoot farmer plowing his field near St. Anthony Falls on the Mississippi River. His axe is driven into a tree trunk, and his rifle and powderhorn are nearby. An Indian on horseback rides into the scene in front of a fiery sunrise. The bottom of the outer ring contains the date 1858, the year that Minnesota gained statehood.

Minnesota even has a state muffin: blueberry. A third-grade class from the northeastern city of Carlton proposed the new symbol in 1988 during a school lesson in how a bill becomes a law. They justified their selection of a state food on the basis of the muffin's all-Minnesota ingredients. Wild blueberries abound in the northland, the students knew, while farmers across the state grow wheat. The young scholars might also have added that from 1880 until 1930, Minnesota—specifically, the short stretch of land along the Mississippi River just below the Falls of St. Anthony in Minneapolis—was the flour-milling center of the world!

Other states have their official flowers, beverages, insects, tartan plaids, and even breeds of horses. But one of the most unusual state symbols is Minnesota's official state photograph, named in 2002. Now world famous, the photo was taken in Bovey, Minnesota, in 1918 by Eric Enstrom. The picture shows an elderly man, his head bowed over a table set with a loaf of bread, a bowl of soup, and a large book. The model, Charles Wilden, was a

Celebrating the centennial of Minnesota Territory, Jackson High School majorettes pose with the Minnesota Territorial Seal, Jackson, Minnesota, 1949. The picture on the seal has been redrawn several times.

poor door-to-door salesman who lived in Bovey. Enstrom called his photograph *Grace.*

During World War II, Enstrom sold the copyright of the photo to a religious publishing company because he was unable to keep up with the many requests for prints. The popularity of the picture came from what seemed to be its sacred content: saying grace before

Willie Walleye is a roadside attraction in Baudette, Minnesota.

This 2007 Minnesota souvenir nail file features many Minnesota emblems and symbols: a map, the state seal, a Norway pine, a loon, the pink and white lady's-slipper, the State Capitol, and the state flag.

a humble meal, a source of spiritual comfort in hard times. Recently some people have objected to including *Grace* on the list of Minnesota emblems. They argue that the book is a Bible and the message is therefore a Christian one, although this is a state of great religious diversity. But a member of the legislature has collected evidence that the book in the photo was a dictionary. *Grace,* she says, actually endorses universal literacy.

"The Mother of Seas"

Without its unique geographical features, Minnesota would have no claim to its many state symbols. There would be no milk or muffins, no flour mills or lady's-slippers, no walleye or loons. Tens of thousands of years ago, this region of North America proved especially vulnerable to the beneficial effects of slow glacial movement.

The back-and-forth travels of glaciers up to a mile thick scooped out Minnesota's existing lakes. They created the iron ore ranges in the northern part of the state and deposited the distinctive soil of the Great Anoka Sand Plain. They carved the fertile valley of the Minnesota River and left a waterfall higher and wider than Niagara Falls downstream from the present site of the Falls of St. Anthony in Minneapolis. Although the map today shows a landlocked state at the center of the continent, Minnesota is also known as the "Mother of Seas" because of the sheer volume of pure Minnesota water that finds its way north into Hudson's Bay, east into the St. Lawrence Seaway, and south into the Gulf of Mexico. Thanks to its roving glaciers, the *topography* (land forms) of Minnesota is spectacularly unique.

Grace is the official state photo. This version has been hand-colored in oil.

Minnesota's land forms also make the state uniquely suited to agriculture. But that's not what critics thought 150 years ago. Back in the 1850s, it was generally believed that the 49th parallel of latitude—an imaginary line on the map that now defines the U.S./Canadian border, except for that strange bump in Minnesota known as the Northwest Angle—was the northernmost point at which it was possible to raise crops. A writer for *Harper's New Monthly Magazine* in 1875 further stated that the western edge of Minnesota was the absolute "limit of successful agriculture."

Apples were a sign of a good growing climate, but many Easterners doubted that the fruit could ever be raised in chilly Minnesota. Skeptics included Horace

Greeley, editor of the *New York Tribune* and the man who coined the phrase, "Go West, young man! Go West!" But in 1855, at an agricultural fair held in Minneapolis, a Connecticut missionary living on the shores of Lake Calhoun brought along three homegrown apples. On later visits to Minnesota, Greeley was forced to eat his words, along with the crisp Minnesota apples that put older New England varieties to shame.

Other myths about Minnesota have been debunked through the decades. Fifty years ago, most grade-school textbooks began with heroic scenes of French priests and explorers "discovering" Minnesota in the 1600s. But Minnesotans now know differently. For all their daring, the French had only found what others already knew about Minnesota.

The Statehood Centennial

In 1958, a Statehood *Centennial* (100th anniversary) Commission held several events to highlight the unique characteristics of the North Star State. Speeches were given. Pageants were held. Special license plates were issued. A queen was crowned. An official song—"They Named It Minnesota"—was written and sung. A "Parade of the Century," which ended at the State Fairgrounds, was led by General Lauris Norstad, a Red Wing native then in charge of NATO forces in Europe. And a centennial train filled with historical artifacts visited eighty-six of Minnesota's eighty-seven counties. (The only reason Cook County was skipped was because it had no railroad tracks!)

The train was the most elaborate and expensive of all the centennial projects. The museum-on-wheels was

moved from town to town by locomotives borrowed from ten railroads. The journey began in Winona in the spring of 1958 and ended in Shakopee in early autumn. It was viewed by more than 600,000 visitors during its 133 days of operation. Five specially remodeled cars contained walk-through exhibits showing "every aspect of Minnesota life—past, present and future." Among the topics of the exhibits were history, resources, agriculture, industry, and "social progress." "Special effects" were part of some of the exhibits. In the agriculture car, for example, fans blew the scent of alfalfa through the air. The portion of the resources display that described Minnesota's woods and wildlife smelled of pine.

When visitors left the train, they were given a thirty-one-page booklet that explained the meaning of the artifacts they had just seen. The astonishing thing about the souvenir booklet was its point of view about the Dakota, Ojibwe, and other Native Americans who were Minnesota's first citizens. The booklet said that Indians were "savages" who were inferior to early Minnesota's white newcomers. The booklet and exhibits, as well as the pageants and ceremonies held along the centennial train's tracks, still reinforced the white version of the state's settlement. It still promoted *Manifest Destiny*—the nineteenth-century belief that white Americans were entitled to occupy all of North America, with no thought given to the injustice done to the native population. "Civilization," to white Americans, meant wiping out or removing these first occupants of Minnesota's pine forests and rivers.

For the most part, Minnesota in 1958 was content

The idea for Minnesota's centennial train was borrowed from the Freedom Train of 1947–1949, which carried 127 historic documents across America, including the Declaration of Independence, the Constitution, the Bill of Rights, and the German and Japanese surrender documents that ended World War II. The train encouraged reflection on America's freedoms at the dawn of the nuclear age.

with its view of Manifest Destiny. It was happy with its booming industries, its fertile fields, and its educational opportunities. So when visitors wrote letters of complaint to the Centennial Commission, it was the little things that troubled them. Some said the lines to enter the train were too long. Others said the train should be cleaner. The display predicting the destiny of Minnesota angered a state senator from Albert Lea, who thought that too much emphasis was placed on urban areas, like the Twin Cities, and on big institutions, like the University of Minnesota. The art show had too much "modern stuff" for folks expecting pretty pictures of Minnesota's heroes and natural beauties.

Yet some Minnesotans did have a bigger complaint about the 1958 centennial. That complaint involved how politics and religion were portrayed in the *emblem* (logo) used by the commission. The emblem appeared prominently on the centennial train and on books and brochures issued by the state during 1958. It also decorated key rings, matchbooks, and other novelty items meant to call attention to the celebration. The emblem's design had been chosen in a contest won by Will Schaeffer, a Minneapolis commercial artist. The guidelines for the contest—which offered a $150 prize—stated that the winning entry should be forward-looking and should represent the diversity of the state's many ethnic groups.

Revisions to Schaeffer's sketch were requested right from the start. First, he had to erase a rocket ship of the future so it wouldn't insult the railroads that had sponsored the centennial train. Then he had to change some modernistic buildings in a futuristic city

Ten-year-old David Robertson of rural Brainerd received a Lionel replica of the centennial train because he was the 500,000th visitor.

to a flour mill. In the end, his emblem consisted of a circle divided in half. The left side showed a woman with a prim hairdo, a silo, a barn, and the year "1858"; the right side showed a contemporary man, the mill, a church steeple, and the year "1958." Almost from the day it appeared, the emblem was criticized for including a Christian cross on top of the steeple.

The problem was that the emblem didn't follow the separation of church and state according to the First Amendment to the U.S. Constitution. The cross, it was said, implied that Minnesota approved of Christianity but not the other faiths practiced in the state. The battle was waged in the "Letters to the Editor" pages of newspapers from St. Paul to St. Cloud, from Roseau to Rochester. "Are we not considered a Christian nation?" asked a Minneapolis woman in favor of keeping the cross. Another correspondent said that "Jewish citizens, in good conscience, will not be able to participate in many aspects of the Centennial" without a change in the design. Others suggested changing the cross into a tree so that no one would be offended. As for the artist, he said that the steeple was simply his attempt to create a visual balance

A ceramic trivet made in Red Wing, Minnesota, pictures the state's centennial emblem. It was one of many souvenirs of the yearlong event.

for the tall silo on the other side of the circle. In the end, the cross stayed.

Celebrating Minnesota's 150th

As the *sesquicentennial* (150th anniversary) of Minnesota's statehood takes place, how differently will Minnesotans see themselves than they might have during the state's centennial? Is the Minnesota of 2008 the same as the Minnesota of 1958? Who and what have made Minnesota such a special place? How will the 150th anniversary celebration differ from that of the 100th?

The Sesquicentennial Commission appointed by Governor Tim Pawlenty has selected four major themes to guide yearlong and statewide 150th observances: Education, Innovation, Arts and Culture, and Health and Wellness. In addition, the commission plans to shine a spotlight on Minnesota's natural resources and our unique outdoors heritage.

Suppose you were a member of the Minnesota Sesquicentennial Commission in 2008. What would you do? Promote Minnesota's official state muffins? Commission a statue or monument? Open a sesquicentennial booth at the Minnesota State Fair?

Great Northern Diver (loon) by naturalist and painter John James Audubon from *The Birds of America.* An original edition of the book, published in sections between 1827 and 1838 and known as the "Double Elephant Portfolio," sold at auction at Christie's in March 2000 for $8,802,500, a world record for any printed book.

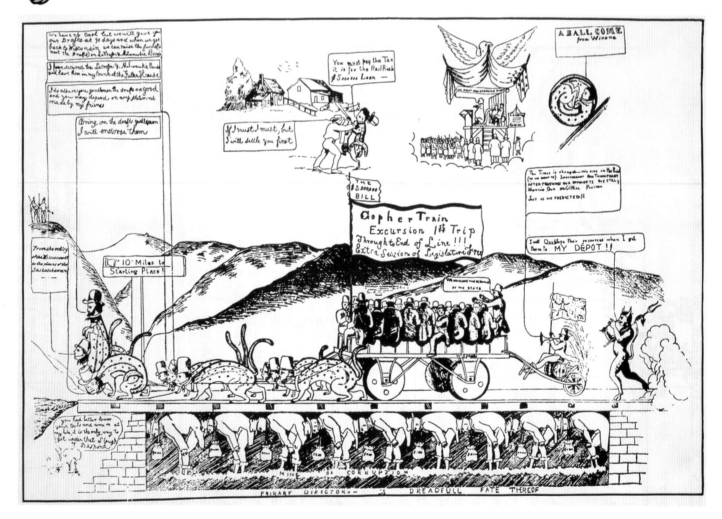

ONE OF MINNESOTA'S nicknames is "The Gopher State." Even before statehood was achieved, Minnesotans argued over whether the gopher or the beaver should be the state mascot.

Supporters of the beaver called gophers useless and destructive. Indeed, in 1857 the Territorial Legislature passed a bill calling for the organized obliteration of gophers and blackbirds as menaces to crops. But gopher defenders observed that beavers were unsuitable as a mascot because they had been hunted almost to extinction. And the few remaining beavers lived mainly up north.

What seems to have settled the matter was an 1858 political cartoon by R. O. Sweeny making

This widely circulated political cartoon by R. O. Sweeny earned Minnesota the nickname "the Gopher State."

fun of lawmakers for passing a bill that authorized $5 million in loans to railroads if they promised to build their lines through Minnesota. The railroads were never completed, the money disappeared, and the matter remained a sore point for decades. Sweeny's cartoon showed a railcar full of gullible legislators being pulled down the track by nine hat-wearing gophers. The gophers stood for the railroad tycoons who had duped the State Legislature. And, although the satire was biting, the gophers were so cute that they proved irresistible!

Cute or not, gophers were the first animal research subjects used by medical students at the University of Minnesota back in 1892. Since then, the gopher has become the semiofficial mascot of University of Minnesota sports. Or is "Goldy Gopher" actually a chipmunk? Or a type of thirteen-lined ground squirrel? Seems nobody really knows for sure.

"hail! minnesota"

MINNESOTA'S STATE SONG, adapted from the University of Minnesota anthem, describes the natural wonders of the state in its beautiful second verse, added in 1905 by U of M student Arthur Upson.

Like the stream that bends to sea,
Like the pine that seeks the blue,
Minnesota, still for thee,
*Thy sons are strong and true.**
From thy woods and waters fair,
From thy prairies waving far,
At thy call they throng,
With their shout and song,
Hailing thee their Northern Star.

*Note: Minnesota's daughters have been called upon in the first verse.

Minnesota legislators singing the proposed state song in 1931. "Hail! Minnesota" was finally adopted as the state song in 1945.

Canoe of Indians, painting by Eastman Johnson, 1857. These Ojibwe lived near Grand Portage, in what is now Minnesota, on the north shore of Lake Superior at the Canadian border.

chapter one

BIRTHPLACE? OF AMERICA?

BETWEEN THE 1600s and 1783, the year that America's Revolutionary War ended, no fewer than four nations claimed the land that is now Minnesota: first France, then England and Spain, and finally the United States. But before that, Minnesota belonged to the First Nations—the Native Americans who lived throughout North America for centuries before European explorers arrived.

But did anyone live in Minnesota before the Native Americans? How long ago did they live here? Could Minnesota be the birthplace of America?

Cavemen and Vikings

Humans have lived in North America for at least 13,000 years, maybe longer. Researchers believe the oldest North Americans are ancestors of modern Native Americans. Did the oldest North American live in Minnesota?

In 1931, while building a highway near Pelican Rapids, Minnesota, construction workers discovered the bones of a teenage girl. The girl may have drowned in a nearby lake that was even older than Glacial Lake Agassiz, a massive body of water that once covered 365,000 square miles in central North America. Known originally as "Minnesota Man" despite her gender, the girl lived 10,000 to 20,000 years ago. Her remains are the oldest to be found in Minnesota and may be the oldest found in North America. The next oldest Minnesotan could be the "Browns Valley Man," whose remains are 8,000 to 10,000 years old. They were found in 1935 in southern Minnesota between Traverse and Big Stone Lakes. The Browns Valley Man was buried among flint artifacts, which suggests that he used tools like those of the early Indians.

In 1976, responding to much petitioning, the Minnesota Legislature correctly renamed the "Minnesota Man" the "Minnesota Woman."

The Jeffers petroglyphs are thought to span some 5,000 years, from 3000 B.C. to A.D. 1750. They depict important events in the lives of the Indians, including religious ceremonies, and emphasize the importance of animals and hunting in their culture.

Other early Minnesotans lived out on the prairies north of Windom, where someone carved almost 2,000 images into a sheet of red bedrock. Archaeologists think many of these *petroglyphs* (rock carvings) are more than 2,000 years old. The petroglyphs show hunters using *atlatls* (levers) to throw spears at wild game, just as other prehistoric inhabitants of North America did long before the Indian bow and arrow were invented.

But the most controversial of all these shadowy early Minnesotans are the "8 Swedes and 22 Norwegians" who left a message on a stone tablet in Kensington, Minnesota, back in 1362. The tablet was discovered in 1898, tangled in the roots of an aspen tree on the farm of Olof Ohman, a Swedish immigrant. The brief message was carved on the stone in *runes* (ancient Scandinavian letters). The message said that ten of the group's thirty men had been killed. The rest were preparing to retreat to their ships, a journey that would take them fourteen days.

While many believed the Kensington runestone was a clever *forgery* (fake), others hoped that descendants of the *Vikings* (explorers from Scandinavia) really *had* come to Minnesota more than a century before Columbus arrived in the New World in 1492. Defenders of the stone's authenticity pointed out that Farmer Ohman seemed to attach no particular cash value to his find. In fact, he was using the stone as the threshold for his barn!

Minnesota's many Scandinavian immigrants were elated by the find, of course. In 1948 the Kensington runestone was displayed at the Smithsonian Institution in Washington, D.C., and photographed for *National Geographic* magazine. Minnesota governor Luther Youngdahl, of Norse descent himself, unveiled the stone with great ceremony at the territorial centennial celebration of 1949. The runestone also was part of the Minnesota exhibit at the New York World's Fair in 1964. In 1951 the Kiwanis Club put up a replica five times the size of the original stone. And the city of Alexandria, Minnesota, the seat of the county in which the stone was found, declared itself the "Birthplace of America" and built a giant statue of a Viking and a museum to prove it.

Opinion continues to be divided about the Kensington runestone. Some say that, given the later adventures of canoe-paddling French voyageurs in North America, "8 Swedes and 22 Norwegians" might have made their way to the future site of the Ohman farm. They could have sailed into Minnesota via Hudson's Bay, the Nelson River, Lake Winnipeg, and the Red River. Recent testing of the stone and new studies on the history of runes have scholars wondering: Could Minnesota be the birthplace of America?

The Kensington runestone in the Runestone Museum in Alexandria may prove that Vikings "discovered" Minnesota in 1362, more than one hundred years before Columbus discovered America.

Proud Alexandrians also erected a monumental statue of the world's largest Viking. Have your picture taken with Big Ole, who stands a whopping twenty-eight feet tall!

First Nations

Scholars believe that the First Nations people of Minnesota are descendants of the state's prehistoric population. In Minnesota, the dominant Indian tribes became the Ojibwe (who were also called the Chippewa) and the Dakota (who were also known as the Sioux). Evidence suggests that the Ojibwe tribes arrived after the Dakota, after gradually being pushed west by the thirteen colonies that established themselves along the Atlantic Coast in the seventeenth century.

Although European writers, including Jean Jacques Rousseau, painted a picture of Indians as simple children of nature living happily in peace, warfare was a part of North American life long before white men arrived from across the ocean. The Ojibwe and Dakota were mortal enemies. (In fact, *Sioux* means "poisonous snake" in the Ojibwe language.)

The cultures of the different Indian bands and tribes were complex, ancient, and fragile. Those who lived in Minnesota at the time the first Europeans arrived led

Dacotah Village by Seth Eastman, ca. 1850. Dakota villages were located close to rivers or lakes and consisted of ridge-roofed houses made of a framework of poles lashed together. Slabs of bark peeled from elm trees were used to cover the walls and roofs of these structures, which ranged in length from twenty to thirty feet and in width from fifteen to twenty feet.

hard lives. They had to depend on the land for their food, clothing, and shelter. They lived in lodges called wigwams, which they covered in bark, or they lived in tipis, which they covered in animal skins. They harvested wild rice and made sugar from the sap of the maple tree. Above all, they hunted. They followed the path of the seasons, moving their villages from place to place in search of buffalo, deer, fish, and geese.

In time, however, the buffalo moved on, away from the hunters. The fur-bearing animals retreated west toward the Rockies. Every change brought difficulties for the Indian and his traditional way of life. No change was more devastating than the arrival of the Europeans.

French Voyageurs

As early as 1534, French adventurers began to explore the rivers of North America, which they called New France. Quebec, now a part of Canada, was formally colonized by France in 1608, a dozen years before pilgrims from England landed on Plymouth Rock on the Massachusetts shore. But with the crowning in 1643 of France's Louis XIV—the "Sun King"— Frenchmen in search of fame and fortune began a vigorous push into the unknown interior of the continent.

Fame would be the prize for the explorer who finally found the fabled water route to China—the same route that Christopher Columbus had been looking for in 1492. Fortune would come from selling furs, or "soft gold." Fur was sold as a luxury item in the capitals of Europe, where fashion called for fur trim on clothes and beaver pelts were made into fine felt hats. Fur was also the currency of the frontier. In exchange for

furs the Frenchmen gave the native peoples cloth, blankets, iron tools, kettles, and modern weaponry.

In North America, the headquarters of the huge, multi-national trade in furs was Grand Portage. This tiny bay in northern Minnesota is just below the spot where the Pigeon River tumbles into Lake Superior. Grand Portage remained an important meeting place between the Europeans, Indians, and EuroAmericans for

This dramatic Carl Bertsch illustration of hardy French fur traders appears in historian Grace Lee Nute's book *The Voyageur.*

The Annual Cycle by artist Howard Sivertson pictures the fur trading enterprise that flowed through a small outpost on the western end of Lake Superior called Grand Portage. Europeans prized the lush furs, some of which they shredded and made into felt for gentlemen's hats.

almost three hundred years. It was the westernmost point where goods could be delivered from the East via water routes. The goods were loaded into giant Montreal canoes. Each boat was thirty-six-feet long and capable of carrying four tons of shirts, caps, needles, gunpowder, flour, whiskey, and whatever else could be bartered for bales of furs. Back in Montreal, these goods had been packed into parcels called "pieces." Each *voyageur* (traveling employee of the fur company) was expected to carry eight such pieces, weighing ninety pounds apiece, up the steep trail that bypassed the treacherous falls of the Pigeon River. The nine-mile trail was the *portage* (overland bypass of rough water). First, the men carried their heavy bales up the trail, one or two at a time. Then they carried their canoes, lighter vessels used on the rivers and streams inland of the Great Lakes. Finally, they came back again, with four bales of precious furs.

The French Canadian voyageurs, dressed in the colorful sashes that doubled as carrying devices for their packs, have passed into Minnesota legend, thanks to the stirring tales of Grace Lee Nute. Nute was a distinguished historian and long-time manuscripts curator at the Minnesota Historical Society. In her book series on these hardy men, beginning with *The Voyageur* in 1931, she tells of the *pork-eaters* (newcomers) who paddled from Montreal to Grand Portage and back. She recalls the *hivernants* (experienced voyageurs) who wintered in the interior, gathering furs from the Indians and living among them. She describes the songs of the voyageurs, the pea soup they ate for every meal, their pipes, and their great strength and endurance.

The Canoe Builders of Saganaga by Howard Sivertson. Friendly native Indians who taught the traders most of the skills they needed to survive and prosper in the wilderness also made canoes for them before the fur companies built their own canoe factories.

The fur trade not only introduced the early industrial age to North America, it changed the culture of the Native Americans forever. When Indians received guns for furs, for example, it became easier for them to make war or to kill more game than they could use. Kettles, along with barrels of pork and beef, changed the foods they ate and prepared. Treaties that promised them *annuities* (regular payments of goods, credit, or cash) in exchange for their lands increased their dependency on the EuroAmericans' merchandise. Even changes in white men's fashions affected the Indians' way of life. When Europeans abroad began to wear hats made of Chinese silk instead of beaver, fur was no longer desired by the traders.

The whiskey that became the standard item of trade with the Indians caused them devastating and lasting damage. It loosened the ties that once bound the members of a tribe. Samuel Pond, a Connecticut missionary who lived among Minnesota's Dakota for decades beginning in the 1830s, would later write that the Indians became violent only after they were given whiskey: "When the Dakotas were sober, murders were not very common among them."

Early *ethnographers* (cultural scientists) like Frances Densmore, the Minnesota woman who began her study of Ojibwe music in the 1890s, were convinced that unless they acted quickly with camera and phonograph, an ancient tribal culture would disappear before their eyes.

The British Are Coming!

Grand Portage and the trading posts it served welcomed men other than the voyageurs: Scottish entre-

preneurs, mixed-blood traders and their families (called *métis*), and Native Americans seeking help or credit between shipments of furs. Eventually, the men included English soldiers and American government representatives from far-off Washington, D.C.

In 1760, after an epic battle between British and French armies on the Plains of Abraham outside Quebec City, France lost its lands east of the Mississippi to England. In a secret treaty, however, France gave Spain the lands that lay west of the river, including a large chunk of what is now Minnesota. But Spanish control meant little or nothing on the frontier. Even when the British claimed *sovereignty* (supreme power) over the United States, French traders continued to bring goods to the western shore of Lake Superior and across the chain of lakes and rivers that

"Song catcher" Frances Densmore was a music teacher from Red Wing, Minnesota, who helped preserve Native American music.

Eastman Johnson's *Grand Portage,* 1857. An American artist trained in Dusseldorf, Germany, Johnson would become famous in the East in the 1860s and 1870s for his paintings of country people: haymakers and cornhuskers, cranberry pickers and maple sugar makers.

led from Montreal into Minnesota. French was still the language of commerce and French names still identified the landscape. Children of French-speaking fathers and Native mothers were among the key people in the early saga of the state of Minnesota.

According to the peace treaty that ended the Revolutionary War of 1776, British lands became part of the new United States of America. International commerce went on as before, however, dominated by the French even when the British and then the Americans were officially in control of the fur trade.

The War of 1812 between the United States and Great Britain is best remembered for the enemy's burning of the White House. The real disagreement between the two countries, however, was control of the fur trade and the borderlands between the United States and British Canada. Even after the war ended, the *Union Jack* (British flag) still flew over posts in the U.S. region called the Northwest Territory.

Becoming Minnesota

The U.S. Congress had resolved to settle how these lands would be governed with the Northwest Ordinance of 1787. The law spelled out the requirements for creating new states from the expanse of land north of the Ohio River. In time, six states were carved out of the Northwest Territory, including Minnesota.

As the era of fur trading passed away, many voyageurs and traders became prominent settlers on the Minnesota frontier. Alexander Faribault, Vital Guerin, Joseph Rondeau (or Rondo), and the infamous "Pig's Eye" Parrant each played a role in the history of Fort Snelling and the nearby settlement that would become St. Paul, the capital of Minnesota.

The story of how Minnesota became an American place, and how the many people who fought for its control became Americans, begins in 1819 with the establishment of Fort Snelling at the juncture of the Mississippi and Minnesota Rivers.

RENVILLE COUNTY. Named after Joseph Renville, son of a French father and a Dakota mother. Renville helped translate the French Bible into the Dakota *tongue* (language). He also served as the interpreter for the Stephen Long expedition that explored Minnesota's Red River Valley in 1823.

ZUMBROTA (Goodhue County). This name, taken from the Zumbro River, is a mispronunciation of the French name for the stream *Rivière des Embarras,* or "River of Difficulties." The difficulties consisted of the driftwood in the water that made canoeing dangerous.

ST. LOUIS COUNTY. Named by explorer Pierre Gaultier de Varennes, sieur de La Vérendrye for Saint Louis, King of France from 1226 to 1270.

ROLETTE (Norman County). Named after the notorious Joe Rolette, a mixed-blood representative to the Minnesota Territorial Legislature. In 1857, Rolette hid a bill to move the territorial capital from St. Paul to St. Peter. If passed, the measure would have oriented Minnesota from east to west—like Iowa—and favored agricultural interests over lumbering and trade. By the time the hidden bill was "found," however, it was too late to act upon it. St. Paul remained the capital city of Minnesota.

Fur trader Joe Rolette ran a fur trading post near the Canadian border at Pembina, where he devised the Red River ox cart.

CHANHASSEN (Carver County). From the Dakota phrase for "tree of sweet juice," or sugar maple.

MENAHGA (Wadena County). From the Ojibwe word for "blueberry."

WABASSO (Redwood County). One of many Minnesota place names taken from Henry Wadsworth Longfellow's 1855 poem *Song of Hiawatha*. Ironically, many Indian words were enshrined in Minnesota geography because they came from Longfellow, not directly from Minnesota's Native inhabitants.

EYOTA (Olmsted County). From the Dakota word meaning "greatest."

CALUMET (Itasca County). The French word for the Indian word for a ceremonial pipe.

BUNGO (Cass County). Named for the descendants of the African American slaves Jean and Marie Bonga, whose son, Pierre Bongo, a fur trader, married into the Ojibwe tribe. Pierre's son George, educated in Montreal, also married an Ojibwe woman. George spoke French, English, and Ojibwe fluently and was a much sought-after interpreter.

The Laughing Waters (Minnehaha Falls) by Seth Eastman, ca. 1850; *hahá* is the Dakota word for "waterfalls."

Falls of St. Anthony by Seth Eastman depicts the cataract in wilder days, ca. 1850.

chapter two

THE FORT
THE FALLS
THE RIVER

IN 1803, PRESIDENT Thomas Jefferson bought the Louisiana Territory from France for $15 million. By today's standards, that was a bargain. The "Louisiana Purchase," which included all the land from the Gulf of Mexico to the Rocky Mountains, doubled the size of the United States overnight. French emperor Napoleon Bonaparte needed the money to pay for a war he was planning against Great Britain. President Jefferson wanted the unexplored lands of the West to gain access to the Mississippi at New Orleans, a vital seaport.

Although the Mississippi had not yet been mapped and *exploited* (used) to the fullest, it was already clear that the "Father of Waters" was one of the world's great rivers. So, as explorers Meriwether Lewis and William Clark began their famous journey toward the Pacific, proving that the Far West could be reached by land, President Jefferson dispatched Lieutenant Zebulon Pike (of Pike's Peak fame) northward to find the source of the Mississippi. At the same time, Pike would look for a strategic location for a military fort.

Building Forts

From the time George Washington was president, the U.S. government had built forts to show its ownership of various districts. Finding good, visible sites on which to proclaim American rule was particularly important after the Louisiana Purchase. And it would be important again at the end of the War of 1812, when the British continued to do business on American soil. The fur trade in Minnesota, which was still controlled by the English and the Scots, seemed to require a federal presence on the Upper Mississippi.

When Lieutenant Pike sailed up the Mississippi in 1805 from St. Louis, Missouri, he found the ideal location for a fort. The site was on a *promontory* (high point) 120 feet above the junction of the Minnesota River (called the "St. Pierre," or St. Peter's River) and the Mississippi (called the "Messipi" by the Ojibwe). Pike signed a treaty with leaders of the Dakota, which gave the 100,000-acre site to the U.S. government. As part of the treaty, Pike promised that American traders would give the Indians higher prices for their furs and better goods than the British could provide. Pike bought the land for sixty gallons of whiskey and $200 in trade goods.

No more action was taken until 1817, when Major Stephen Long, who was also an engineer, was sent

Colonel Josiah Snelling, ca. 1820.

Indian agent Lawrence Taliaferro, ca. 1830.

upstream from St. Louis to examine the site that Pike had bought. Major Long's report called the spot ideally located "to control the navigation of the two rivers." Finally, in the blazing August heat of 1819, Lieutenant Colonel Henry Leavenworth arrived on the scene. With him were ninety-eight soldiers (as well as two of their wives and a newborn) who were prepared to build and live in that fort. The soldiers went to work, cutting down trees to build *barracks* (housing for soldiers) on the swampy bottomland on the river's shore. A year later an outbreak of malaria persuaded Lieutenant Colonel Leavenworth to move his men to the towering cliff above to continue their work. By that time, he had been replaced by Colonel Josiah Snelling, who was making his way slowly toward Minnesota from a military post in Missouri.

Before Snelling arrived, however, other notables did: Lawrence Taliaferro ("Toliver"), who would serve as the government's Indian agent for the next twenty years; Henry Rowe Schoolcraft, who would one day discover the true source of the Mississippi; and Lewis Cass, governor of the Michigan Territory, which then included Minnesota. The three men shared a memorable frontier meal of fresh peas, lettuce, beets, and cucumbers grown in the gardens of Fort St. Anthony.

A Frontier Castle

Displeased with both the location and timber construction of the fort being built by Lieutenant Colonel Leavenworth, Colonel Snelling relocated Fort St. Anthony—as Fort Snelling was first called—to the bluff top and constructed a stronghold of native limestone. Like a medieval castle, Fort Snelling sprouted three towers above its lofty walls: a three-story-high southern tower shaped like a hexagon with loopholes for muskets; a round tower that housed cannon; and a northern tower shaped like a pentagon. Rising high above the river valley, Fort Snelling was the most impressive structure built between the Mississippi and the Pacific before the Civil War. For all its military muscle, however, the fort was never attacked. Instead, it became the focus for negotiations with Indian tribes, a magnet for settlers and tourists, and the center of inland trade for the area.

To aid in the fort's construction, soldiers built a sawmill at the Falls of St. Anthony, the future site of Minneapolis, which in effect created Minnesota's lumber industry. They also built a stone *gristmill* (a building where grain is ground into flour), which paved the way to Minnesota's rank as the flour-milling capital of the world. An 1823 visitor reported seeing more than 200 acres of land around Fort Snelling planted in oats, corn, and wheat. The crops were the beginnings of the state's agribusiness.

A fine historical novel by Minnesota writer Maud Hart Lovelace describes social life at Fort Snelling in the 1830s and 1840s. Written in 1929, *Early Candlelight* paints a detailed picture of the clothing, the decor, and the imported luxuries of the times as well as the rich mixture of New Englanders, French-speaking

Edward K. Thomas's painting *Fort Snelling Seen from Mendota* shows Henry Sibley's stone house at center, ca. 1850.

Thomas Cantwell Healy's portrait of Henry Hastings Sibley, 1860.

Charles Deas's painting of Henry Sibley's dog Lion in 1841.

métis, immigrants, officers, and gently born wives who made up the community gathered high above the waters of the Mississippi. Many of *Early Candlelight*'s characters are thinly disguised historical figures, including Henry Hastings Sibley, the future governor of Minnesota, and Franklin Steele, the fort's *sutler* (civilian merchant) who owned a mill at St. Anthony Falls and, briefly, Fort Snelling itself. Lovelace vividly illustrates how the fort, the falls, and the great river gave rise to modern Minnesota.

St. Anthony Falls

In 1680, the government of New France was eager to define the borders of Louisiana. It sent out a small band of adventurers to explore the headwaters of the Mississippi and to locate its source. Among the party was Father Louis Hennepin, a Franciscan priest who was born in Belgium. After weeks of paddling north against floe ice, Father Hennepin and two of his companions were captured by the Dakota. The three men spent the rest of the winter in Dakota villages near Mille Lacs, Minnesota. With the coming of summer, when the Indians began their annual hunt for game, Father Hennepin seized the opportunity to slip away, set off down the river, and "discover" a mighty waterfall, which he named after his patron saint, St. Anthony of Padua.

Two years later, Father Hennepin was back in France, where he published an account of his adventures, *Description de la Louisiane,* dedicated to his king, Louis XIV. For many avid readers, this book and subsequent versions of Father Hennepin's travels were their introduction to Minnesota. Yet historians and even some of his fellow citizens found fault with Father Hennepin's book. The good priest, wrote French explorer Robert Cavelier de la Salle (who had sent out the mission in the first place), "will not fail to exaggerate everything." As one of the first Europeans to see the mighty Falls of Niagara, perhaps Father Hennepin did stretch the truth a little in describing the only major waterfall on the 2,350-mile length of the Mississippi River. In his book, the modest sixteen-foot drop of the Falls of St. Anthony became a torrent of forty or fifty feet!

The falls, which the Ojibwe called *Mi-ni-rora* (curling water), had been formed far back in geological

Douglas Volk's *Father Hennepin at the Falls of St. Anthony,* ca. 1905, hangs in the Governor's Reception Room in the Minnesota State Capitol.

history, when the Great River Warren split into two waterfalls at the junction of the Mississippi River and the Minnesota River. Back then, the Falls of St. Anthony, which are now close to downtown Minneapolis, were located near St. Paul and Fort Snelling! Over the course of the centuries, the water's current ate away at the soft sandstone riverbed and the falls backed up toward the north, year by year, until they reached their present position. And though they weren't equal to Niagara Falls in size, St. Anthony Falls inspired similar emotions in those who saw them.

This E. Jaccard and Company silver pitcher was presented by passengers to the captain of the *Lady Franklin* on the Grand Excursion of 1854.

By the 1820s, a new breed of traveler had appeared in America: the tourist. Early tourists made a grand circuit of various scenic spots in the East, including Niagara, the mountains of New York and New England, and the Hudson River Valley. The beauty of each place was determined by its ability to inspire strong emotions in the observer. The best scenery was labeled "sublime" and could arouse awe, wonder, and even terror in the minds of tourists. Often, the quality of the experience was magnified by its superiority to any scenery the Old World might have to offer. The Hudson River, for example, was just as good as the Rhine River in Germany. Niagara Falls beat Europe's cataracts by a mile.

Travelers went west in the 1840s and 1850s armed with a set of high expectations for the Falls of St. Anthony. An organized trip up the Mississippi from Illinois to the falls in 1854 put such romantic notions to the test. Known as the Grand Excursion, the rail and steamboat trip was organized by the railroads to promote new business opportunities in the West. Guests included newspaper reporters, scientists, writers, and other celebrities of the era, including President Millard Fillmore. Curious onlookers gathered in the little towns along the Mississippi riverfront to wave to the former president. Fillmore gave an upbeat speech whenever he was asked.

Everywhere, the excursionists saw evidence of astonishing growth. Villages were fast on their way to becoming booming cities. Real estate values were skyrocketing. Anyone with a little *gumption* (nerve) could make a fortune up north. But there were other reasons to come to Minnesota. "Think of that!" exclaimed a hard-nosed executive. "Ladies at St. Anthony's Falls, where I had anticipated seeing only Indians, bears, catamounts, and other like citizens of a primeval forest." On balance, the group was more impressed with the charm of Minnehaha Falls. The "sublime" qualities of the Falls of St. Anthony, on the other hand, were somewhat diminished by the sawmills along its banks. This was a place for industry, not meditation. One guest poured a flask of salt water from the Atlantic Ocean into the Mississippi just below the falls, symbolizing the future union of East and West Coasts by commerce, industry, and the railroad. And then they all left.

In her memoirs, Harriet Bishop, the missionary/teacher who arrived in the rustic settlement of St. Paul in 1847, included a description of her first glimpse of the famous Falls of St. Anthony. In *Floral Home,* published in 1857, she recalled the moment in almost religious terms: "As I caught my first distant view of the foaming cataract, my entire being was imbued with a new enthusiasm. The very atmosphere seemed to emanate from the Creator's immediate presence—and the flowers seemed to have sprung along our pathway. . . . We felt not the overwhelming awe of Niagara; but calm, delighted, pleasurable admiration."

Finding the River's Headwaters

In 1820, a party of explorers headed by Lewis Cass, governor of the Michigan Territory, which included Minnesota, set off to take stock of the lands beyond

Explorer and historian Henry Rowe Schoolcraft, ca. 1855.

the Falls of St. Anthony. One of these explorers was Henry Rowe Schoolcraft, a promising writer and *mineralogist* (student of minerals). Schoolcraft had a deep interest in the Indians and their probable fate once the riches of the land had been revealed to the world. In other words, he was a young man of divided feelings. On the one hand, he was fascinated by the tribes he had encountered. It was Schoolcraft's writings on Indian life and language that inspired Henry Wadsworth Longfellow to publish his popular epic poem, *The Song of Hiawatha,* in 1855. On the other hand, Schoolcraft was a man of the nineteenth century, a time when expansion and exploitation of resources were common in America.

Governor Cass was an important figure on the national political stage. When he declared that a lake in the north-central section of Minnesota was the spot from which the mighty Mississippi began to flow, Schoolcraft and others kept their doubts to themselves. Schoolcraft named it "Lake Cassina" (now

Giacomo Beltrami thought he had found the source of the Mississippi at a lake near Bemidji, in what is now Beltrami County.

Cass Lake) in the governor's honor and went on to write a *Narrative Journal* of the trip in 1821. Schoolcraft's book provided a vivid account of the natural bounty of Minnesota, laced with predictions that this would prove to be the richest agricultural land in the country.

As Cass had realized, there was great honor attached to finding the true source of the Mississippi River—and proving it. When the *Virginia,* the first steamboat to belch its way upriver from St. Louis to Fort Snelling, tied up below the fort's cliffs, the passengers included Giacomo Beltrami, a political outcast from Italy. Beltrami had dreams of becoming a great explorer—perhaps his nation's new Marco Polo or Christopher Columbus. Beltrami managed to join Stephen Long's expedition, which was headed north and west, but he broke off from his companions to look for the elusive "source." In 1824, after many hardships, he made his way back to Fort Snelling alone, full of wild stories of his exploits. His book, written in French, appeared in New Orleans bookstalls that same year.

Beltrami boasted of having found the true source of the Mississippi at Lake Julia, a small, heart-shaped body of water not far from Bemidji, in what is now called Beltrami County. But Schoolcraft still was not convinced. In 1826 and 1832, he ventured north again on several official trips that gave him the chance to pursue the hunt. On the first trip, he helped to negotiate a treaty with the Ojibwe, exchanging mineral rights on their lands—long before the discovery of Minnesota's Iron Range—for a $2,000 annuity. On the second trip, his expedition administered smallpox

Seth Eastman's watercolor drawing of explorer Henry Schoolcraft at Lake Itasca, ca. 1850. "I caused some trees to be felled," wrote Schoolcraft, "pitched my tent, and raised the American flag on a staff, the Indians firing a salute as it rose."

vaccinations and mapped the terrain. Schoolcraft was sure that this time he would discover the headwaters of the great river. With the help of the party's minister, he even came up with a fancy Latin name for the place: the last letters of *veritas* (truth) and the first letters of *caput* (head) spelled Itasca! Schoolcraft at last paddled toward his prize on July 13, 1832. "What had been long sought, at last appeared suddenly," he remembered. "On turning out of a thicket, into a small weedy opening, the cheering sight of a transparent body of water burst upon our view. It was Itasca Lake—the source of the Mississippi."

By 1834, when Schoolcraft wrote the story of his discovery, Minnesota was a recognizable place on the map. The Falls of St. Anthony had not yet become the greatest engine of industrial progress in the west, but the potential for building grain and lumber and blanket

mills was seen by a new class of frontier entrepreneurs. One such go-getter was painter George Catlin, whose images of the Indians recorded what he felt to be a vanishing race. Catlin came to southwestern Minnesota in 1835 and 1836 to inspect the ancient Indian pipestone quarries there. He went away proclaiming that a steamboat voyage to Minnesota ought to be the next feature of Americans' "fashionable tour." Railroad men of the 1850s were dreaming of a direct connection between Minnesota and the East Coast—perhaps a line from Chicago to Duluth, or a bridge across the Mississippi to carry passengers from the end of the line in Illinois, or a rail corridor north from St. Paul. Picturesque, accessible, and rich in opportunity and adventure, Minnesota was about to boom.

Left: Toh-to-wah-kon-da-pee (Blue Medicine), a Dakota medicine man painted by George Catlin, 1836.

The Great Red Pipe Stone Quarry and Falls.

This stereograph view of the great red pipestone quarry was photographed by William Henry Illingworth, ca. 1880.

the song of hiawatha

HENRY WADSWORTH LONGFELLOW'S *Song of Hiawatha* was the most famous and influential poem of the nineteenth century. Published in 1855, it is a book-length poem that Longfellow hoped would become the great national epic of America. In fact, he modeled the four-beat measure and the frequent repetition of words and sounds on a Finnish epic called *Kalevala.* Longfellow used this style of writing to capture the sound of drumbeats, the solemn style of Indian *oratory* (speeches), and the simplicity of nature. Some critics of the day thought the singsong rhythms were too ordinary, but the public loved it.

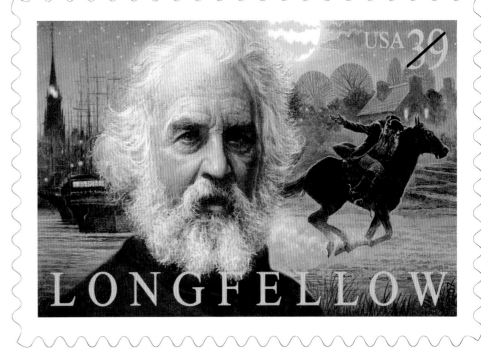

Stereograph view depicting a staged scene from the story of Minnehaha and Hiawatha, ca. 1900.

Jacob Fjelde's life-sized bronze sculpture of Hiawatha and Minnehaha in Minnehaha Park in Minneapolis. The inscription on its base reads: "Over wide and rushing rivers / In his arms he bore the maiden." The sculpture was exhibited at the Chicago World's Fair in 1893.

Longfellow based the setting and the story of Hiawatha, his grandmother Nokomis, and his lady love, Minnehaha, on extensive reading. In particular, he read Henry Rowe Schoolcraft's *History, Condition, and Prospects of the Indian Tribes of the United States*. Longfellow also read Mary Henderson Eastman's popular *Dahcotah; Or, Life and Legends of the Sioux* (1849), which was illustrated with drawings by her husband, Captain Seth Eastman, commander of Fort Snelling. Some Minnesotans quibbled with the *authenticity* (accuracy) of her stories. Missionary Samuel Pond, who also studied the life of the Dakota, declared that the name "Minnehaha [was] neither known nor understood" among the Indians. But Longfellow *appropriated* (borrowed) Mary Eastman's stories to add a dash of romance to his poem.

Tourists already curious about Fort Snelling and St. Anthony Falls began to travel to Minnesota in search of the world of Longfellow. A Hiawatha cult developed around Minnehaha Falls, where a park named in honor of the poet included a replica of Longfellow's house in Cambridge, Massachusetts (now restored), a statue of Longfellow in a *toga* (ancient Greek robe), and a bronze sculpture of Hiawatha carrying Minnehaha across the creek, created in 1893 by Jacob Fjelde. The schoolchildren of Minnesota collected pennies to pay for this lovely tribute to a romantic memory of the state's early days:

"By the shores of Gitche Gumme,
By the shining Big-Sea-Water,
Stood the wigwam of Nokomis . . . "

seth and mary eastman

IN CENTURIES PAST, art was a basic subject studied by cadets bound for the army. Officers were expected to plan forts, draw topography, and sketch out enemy positions. During the 1820s, when Seth Eastman trained at West Point Military Academy, he excelled at topographical drawing. Later, in the 1830s, he taught art there under the direction of the well-known painter Robert Weir.

When Second Lieutenant Eastman served at Fort Snelling, he had a *liaison* (relationship) with a Dakota woman named Stands Like a Spirit. Such liaisons were not uncommon and were regarded as unofficial marriages—at least until the men moved elsewhere or American women arrived on the frontier. The Dakota woman gave birth to Eastman's daughter, Nancy. After his brief stay at Fort Snelling, Eastman moved back East. Nancy Eastman remained behind with her mother and attended a mission school on the shores of Lake Harriet.

In 1841, Colonel Eastman came back to Fort Snelling for a new assignment. He brought with him his wife, Mary, and their three children. Seth and Mary Eastman became prominent *chroniclers* (recorders) of life in Minnesota and its Dakota peoples. Seth painted beautifully detailed watercolors of Native American life and illustrated Henry Rowe Schoolcraft's books. Mary collected and retold tribal stories she heard from Indian women. Several tales concerned Indian maidens wronged by their husbands or fathers. Mary Eastman was often distressed by the unequal treatment of women, white and Indian alike.

Fort Snelling 1848, Head of Navigation by soldier/artist Seth Eastman, who served several stints as commandant at the outpost.

All-wood ox carts from the Red River Valley stream into St. Paul, 1853.

chapter three

FROM TERRITORY TO STATEHOOD

IN THE SUMMER OF 1849, according to official count, fewer than 4,000 people lived in Minnesota. The tally did not include members of the Indian tribes who had called Minnesota home for generations. Nor was it clear at the time just what and where Minnesota was.

Since 1789, when George Washington was elected the first president of the United States, Minnesota appeared on various maps by various names: Indian Territory, part of Louisiana or Missouri, or the west-ernmost part of Illinois or Wisconsin. In 1842, Congress briefly debated whether to make half of Minnesota into an all-Indian state, excluding white settlement. Instead, the land that was left over when Iowa and Wisconsin became states (in 1846 and 1848, respectively) was called Minnesota. And as its changing names suggest, Minnesota was at the cen-ter of the nation's economic ambitions at midcentury.

America's desire for Manifest Destiny pushed through the prairies and forests of Minnesota from two directions. The Lewis and Clark expedition (and the California gold rush of 1849) had demonstrated that Minnesota was no longer the ultimate western boundary of the United States. Instead, it was the midpoint of a crucial corridor linking America's East and West Coasts, from the New England states to Oregon (and, ultimately, to the Orient and its riches). Following inland rivers and chains of smaller lakes, hardy voyageurs paddled mountains of furs and barter goods along this three-thousand-mile trade route. Soon their water highways and canoes would be replaced by iron rails and trains speeding toward the Pacific. Minnesota also linked the nation's North and South. Situated at the northern end of steam-boat navigation on the Mississippi, the city of St. Paul was poised to become one of the country's greatest centers of commerce. And hundreds of wooden ox carts loaded with goods made their way down from the Red River Valley in the north to the warehouses of St. Paul every year, raising hopes that Minnesota might be the staging point for a gradual takeover of Canada's western provinces. If only the "Indian question" could be settled! But the first order of busi-ness was to settle upon a definition for Minnesota.

The Stillwater Convention

Minnesota was no longer part of the Wisconsin Terri-tory, which had ceased to exist when Wisconsin became a state in 1848. As former residents of a territory that no longer existed, representatives of lumber and trading interests decided to petition for rights as U.S. citizens temporarily without standing in Washington, D.C. They met in Stillwater, Minnesota, in August 1848. The Stillwater Convention was Minnesota's first step on the road to statehood. Nobody officially approved of the meeting or voted its delegates into office. They just boldly asserted their claim and sent Henry Hastings Sibley off to Washington as Minnesota's first congressional representative. But the white population he represented was short of the minimum of residents required for becoming a *legitimate* (legally recognized) territory.

Despite this detail, Sibley was surprised to be seated in the House of Representatives as a nonvoting member. Congressmen who had expected a man in moccasins and buckskins were astonished at the eloquent gentleman who argued on behalf of his fellow pioneers. With his passion and charm, Sibley became the chief *advocate* (champion) for Minnesota's statehood, a campaign that began immediately after the Minnesota Territory was proclaimed with the help of Senator Stephen Douglas of Illinois, a leading voice for Manifest Destiny. The bill creating the Minnesota Territory and making St. Paul its capital was signed into law in March 1849. "Thank the Lord!" cried one Minnesota pioneer when the news trickled into the Mississippi Valley a month later. "We live in the United States again!"

Minnesota Territory

Zachary Taylor, the nation's new president and a former commander at Fort Snelling, wasted no time in appointing Alexander Ramsey the first territorial governor of Minnesota. Ramsey was a thirty-four-year-old Pennsylvania lawyer and Taylor's political *ally* (partner). Ramsey's friends in the East teased him on the appointment. Would he go to Minnesota via the Isthmus of Panama, they wondered? Ramsey's wife cried, "Minnesota! Where on earth is it? In Denmark?"

Minnesota territorial governor Alexander Ramsey's buckskin coat with Native American fancywork, ca. 1850.

All jokes and fears aside, the Ramseys arrived in St. Paul by Mississippi steamboat in May 1849. The couple were welcomed by Henry Sibley, who invited them to stay in his house in Mendota for a month. Sibley's stone mansion was the finest private residence in the new Minnesota Territory. It was a place of luxury and grace in the wilderness. There were tall white candles with glass crystals reflecting their every flicker, a harpsichord, silverware, delicate goblets of red glass, heavy linens, and porcelain statuettes of George Washington and his military friend, the Marquis de Lafayette. Its *portico* (columns upholding a triangular shape called a *pediment*) and tall porch echoed the fashionable classicism of East Coast architecture.

Alexander Ramsey, Minnesota's first territorial governor, with his young son, Alexander Jenks Ramsey, ca. 1849.

Governor Ramsey was more eager to identify himself with the West than the East. On June 25, he was paddled across the Mississippi River in a birchbark canoe to begin his duties as a frontier leader. Immediately he set up legislative districts and announced a Minnesota-wide election to be held August 1. In September, Minnesota's first territorial legislature assembled in the dining room of the Central House, a hotel in St. Paul, and received several messages from the new governor. One message is of particular interest because it urges settlement of the extensive Dakota country west of the Mississippi River, a region "superior to any part of the American Continent." The district was rich in timber, meadows, and prairie farmlands, Ramsey wrote, all excellent for the health of potential immigrants. He urged legislators to petition Congress to obtain the region from the "wild" Indian bands who occupied what was called the "Suland."

This watercolor pictures the Sibley House in the late 1880s, by which time its portico had vanished, probably due to rot.

Treaty of Traverse des Sioux

For the go-getters who promoted the wonders of Minnesota in the 1850s, the only roadblock to maximum immigration in the new territory was the presence of Indians. Their tribal wars sometimes spilled into the fields and settlements of white pioneers. Legislators wondered how the native peoples could be contained or removed. With the help of Henry Sibley, who had lived among the Dakota (or Sioux) for twenty years, runners were dispatched in 1851 to announce a great gathering of Upper Sioux tribesmen at Traverse des Sioux for making a new treaty. Traverse des Sioux, a French name meaning a shallow place where the Dakota crossed the Minnesota River, was a traditional Indian meeting ground where traders also conducted business. Located on U.S. Highway 169 near St. Peter, the treaty site was marked in 1914 with a brass plate fixed to a boulder on which the usual gifts for the Indians had been displayed.

This treaty meeting was like the many that went before it, except for the size, pageantry, and sadness of the occasion. Speeches and negotiations were held in an open-air pavilion, with Baltimore artist Frank Blackwell Mayer recording the events much as a television cameraman might: as an eyewitness to history. Gifts

Frank Blackwell Mayer's painting of the *Treaty of Traverse des Sioux,* ca. 1905, hangs in the Governor's Reception Room in the Minnesota State Capitol. The young artist from Baltimore was present at the treaty signing in 1851.

were exchanged. The chiefs dined on beef and pork supplied by the treaty commission. In turn, the Indians staged colorful medicine dances, mock battles, and races for the amusement of the commissioners. By the end of July 1851, however, the time for entertainment was over. Thirty-five chiefs signed their marks on a treaty paper *ceding* (giving) more than 24 million acres of their lands to the United States for a mere seven-and-a-half cents an acre. In return, the Dakota were to receive more presents and promises, including annuities.

Next to the table where the Dakota made their fingerprints on the treaty document was a barrel where the "traders' paper" lay. After each chief signed the first treaty, he was "pulled by the blanket" to the barrel and told to sign once again, thereby agreeing that money promised in the treaty would be used first to settle any debts owing to traders for past advances of food, arms, and other wares. This act of trickery on the part of the traders meant that many Dakota bands would see little if any of their annuity payments. With fur-bearing animals hunted to near extinction, with game fleeing before the white man's guns, and with more and more settlers arriving daily from the East, Indian elders realized they had no choice but to sign whatever treaties were put before them. Their people needed whatever the white man was willing to give.

In the eyes of white settlers, the Indians were too often seen as "pagan savages . . . their breasts filled with a relentless and untamable ferocity," said a journalist of 1875, looking back on those early days. The chiefs who signed the Treaty of Traverse des Sioux were doomed to become a vanishing race, the one

last obstacle to the course of Manifest Destiny. Deceit speeded the process along. Two weeks after the gathering on the Minnesota River, the rest of the Dakota tribes signed a similar treaty at Mendota, Minnesota, completing the deal. (Facing similar pressures, the Ojibwe signed away their lands in 1854 and 1855.) The treaties of 1851, said one of the interpreters, "were as fair as any Indian treaties." But the anger and despair triggered by them would later contribute to the tragic sequence of events known as the U.S.–Dakota War of 1862.

Eyewitness to History

The story of the decisive events of 1851 are known to today's Minnesotans, thanks to the efforts of James Goodhue, a native of New Hampshire. Goodhue arrived in St. Paul in April 1849 aboard the steamboat *Franklin* as soon as the ice went off the waters of the Mississippi River. Determined to be the first to announce the creation of the Minnesota Territory, he set up his hand-operated printing press and recorded the momentous event in the first edition of the *Minnesota Pioneer* only ten days later. Like its successor, the *St. Paul Pioneer Press,* Goodhue's newspaper reported the happenings of the day, including the 1851 treaty meetings at Traverse des Sioux and Mendota. But Goodhue did so in a highly personal way, mixing strong opinions and sensationalism with fact—not to mention ads for new ladies' hats, "Dr. Ford's Pectoral Syrup," and other products of *dubious* (questionable) usefulness.

This mix of passion, fiction, and salesmanship was typical of American journalism in Goodhue's era. Horace Greeley of the *New York Tribune* was well known for having—and printing—his opinions on almost every subject. It was Greeley, for example, who stated as fact that Minnesota was "a barren and inhospitable region, unsuitable for farming, fit only for logging operations." Sentiments like these aroused the anger of Minnesotans and particularly of Goodhue, who had traveled around his new homeland by horseback, riverboat, and canoe. Goodhue had seen potential farms where others saw only barren prairie. The *Minnesota Pioneer,* under Goodhue's management, boasted and boosted to attract newcomers to Minnesota, a place of beauty, "clear bracing air," and "an invigorating winter to give elasticity to the system."

James Goodhue's printing press was built in Cincinnati, Ohio, about 1836. Goodhue printed his first edition of the *Minnesota Pioneer* in St. Paul in 1849.

Goodhue, along with other prominent Minnesotans of his generation, foresaw a great future for the territory and therefore painted its features in dazzling colors.

Their cause was taken up by William Gates LeDuc, who came to St. Paul in 1850, hard on Goodhue's heels. In fact, as a correspondent for Greeley's *New York Tribune,* LeDuc was present with Goodhue at Traverse des Sioux and Mendota for the signing of the Dakota treaties that would open Minnesota to large-scale immigration. LeDuc became Minnesota's principal booster and cheerleader. In 1853 and 1854, the governor appointed him to represent Minnesota's interests at a highly publicized exposition in New York City. This fair was a small-scale copy of London's famous Crystal Palace Exhibition of 1851, the first in a long string of international World's Fairs. Inside London's revolutionary glass-and-iron building, the items on display represented "the works of industry of all nations." New York's smaller fair had more modest ambitions, although it did include among its industrial products a small house constructed entirely of chocolate. How could Minnesota and its official representative—the enterprising young William LeDuc—hope to compete with *that* kind of marvel?

Well, LeDuc did it. After a difficult journey by steamboat and railroad, he arrived in New York with a buffalo in tow! Although the balky animal was confined to a sideshow, LeDuc had much more to offer: Minnesota-grown corn, barley, spring wheat, and wild rice, along with furs trapped on Minnesota soil.

Horace Greeley, LeDuc's former boss, criticized the Crystal Palace show in his newspaper for its disorganized presentation of the nation's business. At the same time, he praised LeDuc extravagantly for his modest but well-chosen display of produce. None of the other territories had sent agricultural products to New York. So, in an editorial published in August 1853, Greeley retracted his former opinion of Minnesota and, according to William LeDuc, "started a tide of immigration to Minnesota." Who cared if other, less noteworthy journalists insisted that Minnesota was an American Siberia, where winters lasted six months and snow piled to twelve feet? Greeley had spoken. Minnesota was a great place for farmers, entrepreneurs, and those in search of the good life.

Building a Boomtown

By the time William LeDuc returned to Minnesota from New York, the cities of St. Paul, St. Anthony, and Stillwater were quickly becoming places of importance. Legislators had already decided to divide the major functions of the Minnesota Territory among the three cities. St. Paul got the capitol, a New England–style brick building with a perky dome on top. St. Anthony (which in 1872 was incorporated into Minneapolis, a made-up Dakota/Greek name) got the University of Minnesota. And Stillwater got the penitentiary, an asset in any frontier district where justice had until recently been of the rough-and-ready kind.

William Gates LeDuc, influential promoter of Minnesota, ca. 1848.

First office of the *Pioneer & Democrat* newspaper in St. Paul, 1858.

Main Avenue of the New York Crystal Palace, where William LeDuc exhibited products of the Minnesota Territory, 1851.

These assets meant that Minnesota was now "civilized." Flour was being milled commercially in Minneapolis. St. Paul was a boomtown, with land prices on the rise, but it also had ice cream shops, a photographer's parlor, and a bowling alley. Agricultural societies sprang up too. Their annual fairs of the 1850s gave prizes to the giant cabbages and turnips that proved the fertility of Minnesota soil. In 1854, in an act of technological *bravado* (defiance), several entrepreneurs led by Franklin Steele built a wire suspension bridge—a toll bridge—across the Mississippi, joining St. Anthony with Minneapolis. The new territorial governor, Willis Gorman, spoke at the dedication

in 1855, and used the occasion to imagine trains tooting across the bridge. The Atlantic and the Pacific would surely meet right here! After Governor Gorman gave his speech, a crowd of unruly but happy drunks burst from the crowd and staggered across the river. Yes, Minnesota had everything: bridges, ice cream, learning, brick buildings—and lots of saloons.

Liquor was a major social problem in the West. During the era of intense fur trading, unscrupulous agents had given spirits to the tribes they visited, often with catastrophic results. In white frontier society, drunkenness was often an answer to dashed hopes and thwarted ambitions. Such was the case with Nininger, Minnesota.

In its prime, the town of Nininger, seventeen miles south of St. Paul, had a baseball team, a dance hall, a plow factory, three hotels, a drugstore, several real estate agents—and six saloons. Founded in 1857, the town was a profit-making venture founded by John Nininger, the brother-in-law of territorial governor Alexander Ramsey, and Ignatius Donnelly. Nininger bought a parcel of land, divided it into lots, laid out streets, and began selling the lots, expecting to grow rich on the profits when the immigrant population in Minnesota exploded. To promote sales of lots, Donnelly "boomed" the new town in a series of posters, ads, and newspapers promising easterners—especially Philadelphians—a paradise in the West.

For a time, everything seemed to go as promised. By the first part of 1858, almost 1,000 people had built homes and businesses in Nininger. Public lectures were offered, parties were held, and more was yet to come. Ads for the town mentioned hotels, a grand library, and fortunes to be made when boats bound upriver stopped at the town docks. But the great bubble of speculation in real estate finally burst. Historians call it the Panic of 1857.

When it spread to Minnesota, the panic took the form of falling land values. People who had bought lots at high prices on easy credit, and were swept along by the promise of ever-rising profits, suddenly found themselves deep in debt for worthless property. Donnelly's ads assumed a bleakly humorous tone: "Cure

The first suspension bridge across the Mississippi River at Minneapolis in 1855, depicted on a collectible plate.

Minnesota's first Capitol, at Tenth and Cedar in St. Paul, 1853.

for the Panic! Emigrate to Minnesota! Where no banks exist!" Within a year, more than half of Nininger's population abandoned their homes or moved them a few miles down the road to Hastings, the county seat, which seemed to be holding up against the financial storm. Soon, only one of Nininger's 3,800 lots was occupied—by Ignatius Donnelly, a fervent believer in his own advertisements. "What a beautiful land has the red man lost," he wrote, "and the white man won." In his own case, Donnelly had won a ghost town. He was a millionaire at twenty-six and a pauper at twenty-seven. He plowed up the rest of the lots, planted wheat, and consoled himself with politics and a new career as a writer.

Although his publications are often criticized today, Donnelly was the Stephen King of mid-nineteenth-century America. His book on the lost continent of Atlantis (1881) went through twenty-one editions. *Caesar's Column: A Story of the Twentieth Century* (1890) sold 700,000 copies. His works fall into two related categories: the utopian—and Nininger was a kind of *utopia* (ideal town)—and the distopian, like the New York City of 1988 he foresaw, with its sci-fi skyscraper of human corpses set in concrete. In exaggerated form, Donnelly's visions of utopia and distopia reflect the two sides of his experience with the building of Nininger, Minnesota. And all of his books—especially those in which he argues by means of a supposed secret code that Shakespeare's plays were written by someone else—show the imagination of a man of affairs in the Minnesota Territory on the eve of statehood.

Dred Scott's Wedding

In 1857, as the bill that would make the Minnesota Territory a state worked its way through Congress, the population was booming. More than 150,000 citizens lived in Minnesota as compared to fewer than 4,000 when Henry Sibley was sent off to Congress.

In excited prose, Donnelly urged settlers to come to Minnesota, 1857.

Ignatius Donnelly, cofounder of the town of Nininger, was also a successful novelist and lieutenant governor. Photo ca. 1865.

Slave Dred Scott based his bid for freedom, which failed, on his residency at Fort Snelling in the 1830s.

Farmers had arrived in astonishing numbers, *displacing* (pushing out) the Dakota and the Ojibwe. Despite recent economic hard times, money could still be made in the businesses headquartered in St. Paul. There was wheat to grind into flour in St. Anthony and trees to be turned into lumber.

In a real way, however, Minnesota's voyageur past and its immediate future as the third largest state in the Union (after Texas and California) had come together at Fort Snelling in 1836. The fort's physician, John Emerson, had brought with him a slave named Dred Scott. Within the year, and with the consent of his master, Scott married a woman named Harriet, who belonged to Lawrence Taliaferro, the local Indian

agent. Taliaferro, who had a reputation for honest dealings with his Indian clients, agreed to sell Harriet to Dr. Emerson. Later, Emerson moved to Missouri, taking the Scotts with him. After his master died, Dred Scott sued for his freedom on the grounds that he had lived in Minnesota, where slavery was forbidden by the Missouri Compromise of 1850. The case eventually reached the U.S. Supreme Court, which declared that a black person was not a citizen, no matter where he lived.

The Supreme Court's 1858 decision led indirectly to the long and bloody Civil War of the 1860s and set the new state of Minnesota on a hard and bitter road to maturity.

St. Cloud anti-slavery editor Jane Grey Swisshelm, 1852.

Swisshelm's home and newspaper office in St. Cloud, ca. 1858.

JANE GREY SWISSHELM arrived in Minnesota Territory in 1857 in search of peace of mind, good health, and freedom from an unhappy marriage. With her six-year-old daughter, she settled in St. Cloud and became editor of the *St. Cloud Visiter.* A strong enemy of slavery, she argued in her editorials and speeches that the practice degraded not only the slaves but also the persons who bought and sold them. She compared the status of the slave with that of the married woman: *disenfranchised* (without rights) and the property of her husband.

As a woman, Swisshelm was not allowed to vote, yet she was influential in founding the Republican Party—the party of Abraham Lincoln—in Minnesota. Not everyone agreed with her, but others in the St. Cloud community rallied to her cause, inspired by her courage and determination. She set an example for the *feminists* (supporters of women's rights) who came after her: women's talents and beliefs were every bit as important as men's.

Like most of us, Jane Swisshelm was a bundle of contradictions. She crusaded for the *abolition* (end) of slavery but called for the extermination of Native Americans. She railed against the elaborate clothing styles favored by women of her generation, yet designed and embroidered a fantastic wedding gown for her daughter. Henrietta Zoe Swisshelm (Mrs. Ernest Allen) marched down the aisle in a dress covered with a design of the plants and flowers of Swisshelm's garden in St. Cloud. Each floral motif had been outlined in infinite numbers of tiny stitches by her mother. The Chicago newspapers, which had followed the Minnesota editor's outspoken views on ladies' costumes, took her to task for the frivolity of the gown, now in the collection of the Minnesota Historical Society. But when Jane Grey Swisshelm's head came into conflict with her heart on this happy occasion, a mother's love won out.

treaty rights and tribal gaming

IN THE 1990s, anglers' objections to spearing and netting traditions of the Mille Lacs Band of Chippewa (Ojibwe) exploded into *hostile* (angry) demonstrations. But the discussion of treaty rights, while a source of anger and apprehension, is also a healthy sign that Minnesotans are now prepared to address the historic divide between Native peoples and the late-comers to the state.

By the mid-1700s, migrating from the Atlantic coast of North America, the Ojibwe had established themselves in the region around Mille Lacs Lake in what is today central Minnesota. They lived off the land by hunting deer, bear, moose, waterfowl, and small game; fishing the area's lakes and streams; gathering wild rice, maple sugar, and berries; and cultivating plants. But all too soon the Mille Lacs Ojibwe were witness to a new presence in their homeland.

Europeans started arriving, and as their numbers grew, they began taking more and more of the Mille Lacs Band's land and natural resources, in violation of treaties and agreements. The newcomers also introduced new diseases, and by the end of the nineteenth century, only a few hundred Ojibwe remained on the Mille Lacs Reservation.

Over the next century, with their traditional way of life changed forever, the Mille Lacs Band struggled with poverty and despair. Finally, in the early 1990s, the band opened Grand Casino Mille Lacs and Grand Casino Hinckley. Since then, casino revenues have allowed the Mille Lacs Band to strengthen its cultural identity, return to economic self-sufficiency, rebuild its reservation, and increase the prosperity of the entire region.

As of 2008, there are fifteen casinos in Minnesota owned by federally recognized Native American tribes. The *autonomy* (self-rule) of reservations and the power of tribal governments to set their own plans of action come from some of the oldest treaties drawn up between Native Americans and EuroAmerican interlopers. After two centuries of mistreatment, the rights of this nation's first citizens are finally being recognized by the law.

Grand Casino Mille Lacs and hotel complex, Onamia, Minnesota.

Howard Pyle's 1906 interpretation of Minnesotans in action at the Battle of Nashville.

chapter four

A TALE OF TWO WARS

THE NATION'S GREAT political battles of the 1850s had hardened around the issue of slavery. Harriet Beecher Stowe's 1852 anti-slavery novel, *Uncle Tom's Cabin,* helped stir up public opinion against the idea that one human being could or should own another. In the South, where slavery was the driving force behind the cotton industry, an attack on the "peculiar institution" of slavery amounted to an attack on the southern way of life and the rights of individual states to regulate their own business. In the North, the debate led to the formation of the Republican Party.

Minnesota and Slavery

In the summer of 1860, Richard Christmas, a Deep South planter, brought his family to Minnesota by steamboat for the season. Southerners wanting to escape their region's summer heat were the most important group of customers at resorts scattered along the Mississippi around St. Anthony Falls, where the breezes were cool and the scenery intoxicating. With the Christmases was Eliza Winston, a female slave who took care of the family's baby. Either at the posh Winslow House, where the Christmases first stopped, or at the house they later rented at Lake Harriet, Eliza Winston met local free blacks. With their

encouragement, she filed suit for her freedom on the grounds that slavery was banned in Minnesota by federal law. Eventually, she made her way to Canada with the blessings of Mr. Christmas and the courts, but not before some Minnesotans attacked the hotel and the vacation house, threatening to tar and feather those responsible for scaring off tourist business from the South. Many also blamed Jane Grey Swisshelm's pro-Republican abolitionist editorials for causing the fuss. Her St. Cloud home was raided and her press dumped in the river.

In the long run, however, politics were probably less important to most Minnesotans than economics. Some business owners in the cities feared competition from cheap or free black labor. A St. Paul headline of 1857 pitted "White Supremacy against Negro Equality." But in rural areas, where Republicans were strongest, newly arrived immigrant farmers, generally conservative in outlook, were opposed to slavery on moral grounds. They also tended to be Prohibitionists, alarmed by the consequences of hard drink. The terrible effects of liquor distributed to the native population especially angered Henry Benjamin Whipple, the first Episcopal bishop of Minnesota. He wrote to a federal Indian agent shortly after his 1859 arrival, urging special concern for the Dakota. "We have dispossessed them," Whipple argued, "blasted [their] home by the accursed firewater." The future of slavery and the fate of the Dakota would become Minnesota's major concerns in the 1860s.

In the spring of 1861, Governor Alexander Ramsey went to Washington, D.C., for the inauguration of Abraham Lincoln, the nation's newly elected president. Governor Ramsey was still in the nation's capital on April 12, seeking government aid to combat the effects of the recent financial panic, when Southern troops attacked and seized Fort Sumter in the Charleston harbor of South Carolina. America's bloody Civil War had begun. Immediately, Ramsey pledged 1,000 Minnesota volunteers to the cause, even before President Lincoln issued a call for troops. Using the new telegraph connection to St. Paul, Ramsey ordered his lieutenant governor, Ignatius Donnelly, to assemble recruits. Within days, more than 1,000 men had lined up at Fort Snelling to volunteer. Minnesota thus became the first state to answer the national call to arms. The First Minnesota Regiment, already practicing drills at the fort in May, was the first to enlist for a three-year hitch in the Union Army.

Officers of the First Minnesota Volunteers (and their guests) gather at Fort Snelling, 1861.

Why Men Fought

Opposition to slavery was not what brought Minnesotans to enlist at Fort Snelling. In fact, the Minnesota Legislature had recently debated whether to allow slaveholders to visit the state for several months without forfeiting the right to keep their slaves. The 24,000 Minnesota men who eventually served the Union with great distinction were driven by a variety of reasons. Some historians point to the soldiers' desire to preserve the Union that Minnesota had so recently joined. Others observe that many young men sought glory and relief from the chores of daily life. But the state was now an important part of the United States. Thanks to the telegraph and faster means of transportation, America's problems were also Minnesota's problems. A wave of patriotism washed over Minnesota in April and May 1861, sweeping up volunteers, supporters, and the public at large.

Minnesotans flocked to Fort Snelling, eager for a glimpse of the new soldiers. The ladies of Winona worked feverishly to sew gray uniforms and a splendid battle flag for hometown boys who enlisted. The state bought suitable outfits for the rest: red flannel shirts with black pants, hats, and suspenders. (Only in August, after their first taste of combat, was the First Minnesota given the standard blue uniform to wear. The red ones made easy targets!) Civilians ringed the parade grounds of the fort, bringing gifts of all sorts. As preparations went forward, Governor Ramsey selected former territorial governor Willis Gorman, a veteran of the Mexican War, as the colonel of the regiment.

Expecting this latest war to be a brief adventure, the Minnesotans set off for Washington in high spirits

Former territorial governor Willis A. Gorman served with the First Minnesota Infantry in the First Battle of Bull Run in July 1861.

Knute Nelson posing in his Civil War uniform in 1862 represents the new European immigrants who fought in Minnesota's war effort.

he wrote, "riddled with cannon ball, buck-shot and bullets" from the engagement at Bull Run. On behalf of the state, Governor Ramsey expressed thanks for "the virgin white battle flag of our 'Northern Light' of the American Union." The road to the Confederate surrender at Appomattox in 1865 would be long and hard won.

By the end of 1862, after news of the frightful toll of dead and injured spread, volunteers were few. A draft order issued in March 1863 called for all able-bodied men between the ages of twenty and forty-five to report to duty. Draftees, however, were given the option of buying substitutes to fight for them, leading to further disillusionment. Was this a rich man's war in which only the poor were fated to die? In 1864, as the conflict dragged on, a St. Paul newspaper reported that most of the Minnesota substitutes had been destitute Ojibwe Indians and mixed bloods.

by steamboat and train, arriving just in time for the shocking defeat of the Union forces at the First Battle of Bull Run in July 1861.

In Battle

In that demoralizing skirmish—the first real clue that the war would not be a brief picnic with medals for all—the First Minnesota was one of the only units to hold its position on the right end of the Union line. They did so at a terrific cost. One in five of the brave young men who had set off from Fort Snelling only three weeks earlier was killed or wounded by the time the victorious General Pierre Beauregard left the field of battle. On July 31, Colonel Gorman sent his unit's flag back to the ladies of Winona. It was now,

Minnesota's regiments served with distinction in some of the most celebrated clashes of the Civil War. At Gettysburg, in 1863, the First Minnesota held Cemetery Ridge, bore the brunt of Pickett's Charge, and, according to some authorities, won the battle that turned the tide of the war. Of 262 men on the line, all but 47 were killed or wounded. Other Minnesota regiments took part in victories at Nashville, Vicksburg, Missionary Ridge, and Corinth. Corinth was a key railhead in Mississippi. The Fifth Minnesota engaged in a fierce battle there in October 1862, with the spiritual support of young John Ireland, chaplain of the regiment and future archbishop of St. Paul. Ireland won the loyalty of his men for tending to the wounded, playing chess with soldiers between hostilities, and passing ammunition in the heat of battle. Afterward, in the genteel language typical of the period, Ireland praised the Fifth for its gallantry under fire: "With what unanimity, with what rapidity, what visible coolness and unflinching courage they poured volley after volley into the ranks of their opponents!"

Comrades in Arms

It is estimated that one in ten Minnesota men fought in the Civil War. Many never came home. But for those who did, the *camaraderie* (fellowship) forged in battle among men of different backgrounds, professions, and countries of origin was one of the most important consequences of the conflict. Soldiers who spent their youth far from home formed bonds with their messmates, their officers, and their chaplains that continued into civilian life. Their leadership would dominate the state for the rest of the century. Their generation also raised impressive monuments to their role in preserving the Union.

Father John Ireland, the future Catholic archbishop of St. Paul, served as a chaplain to Minnesota troops in 1862.

Samuel D. Badger, a drummer boy for the First Minnesota. Drummers as young as eleven beat out signals during battles.

On July 2, 1897, the state erected on Cemetery Ridge at the Gettysburg battlefield a granite base topped by the statue of a Minnesota private charging forward, his bayonet at the ready. The crowd present at the dedication included 165 veterans of the First Minnesota who were sent to Pennsylvania at state expense to observe the thirtieth anniversary of their deeds. The plaque beneath the bronze soldier reads: "A Regiment with a Reputation. As the Union line reeled back on July 2, 1863, 262 men of the First Minnesota charged Confederates advancing over the low ground ahead and saved the day. They suffered 82 percent casualties—believed to be the highest regimental loss in any battle, in proportion to the number engaged, in modern history."

That text was typical of the public tributes paid to the Civil War veterans of Minnesota. Many former officers, for example, wrote stirring *memoirs* (autobiographies) of their time in uniform and used their military titles for the rest of their lives. William Gates LeDuc—the man who once took a live buffalo to New York on behalf of Minnesota Territory—regarded his service as a brigadier general in the quartermaster corps as the defining time of his life. His book describes his adventures while rushing supplies to battlefields. LeDuc joined thousands of former soldiers who relived their glory days through membership in the Grand Army of the Republic. The GAR was a powerful veterans group that dominated the local and national political scene for several generations.

When Minnesota opened its splendid marble capitol building in 1905, a solemn procession of GAR members carried captured Confederate battle flags from the old building to the new one. The spoils of war included the banner of the 28th Virginia Regiment, seized by Minnesotans at Gettysburg more than forty years earlier. The flag is still a sore point between the two states. Virginia wants it back. Minnesota, with the blessing of the courts, refuses to part with it.

Monument of the First Minnesota Vols. on the Battle Field of Gettysburg, Pa.

Erected by the State of Minnesota on the spot where the Regiment on July 2nd, 1863, made the most famous and successful charge recorded in history, loseing in less than 20 minutes time a little over 82% of its officers and men were killed and wounded

This commemorative postcard remembers the courageous First Minnesota Volunteers at Gettysburg.

Brigadier General William Gates LeDuc at the siege of Chattanooga, with Lookout Mountain in the background.

War at Home

Even as Union Army troops practiced drills and marching at Fort Snelling, rumors of another conflict much closer to home began to circulate. In 1861, when the First Minnesota set off on its journey to Bull Run, the St. Peter newspaper called for military protection for the towns of the Minnesota River Valley. Signs of unrest were evident on the Dakota reservations scattered along the banks of the stream. Tribal affairs were being handled by traders and federal officials concentrated at the Lower Sioux (Redwood) Agency in the south and the Upper Sioux (Yellow Medicine) Agency in the north. What would the farmers and townspeople of the region do, asked the editorial, in case of some "sudden freak of the aborigines" if the fighting men of Minnesota were occupied elsewhere?

White hostility toward Native Americans was already running high in the 1850s when editor James Goodhue of St. Paul cringed at the sight of "wigwams" visible from his office window. "The welfare of the

Indians," he wrote, "requires their speedy removal from a neighborhood that makes them daily more dependent, and in which they learn the vices but attain none of the virtues of civilized life." The treaties of Mendota and Traverse des Sioux had served the purpose of removing wigwams from downtown St. Paul, but they had also taken away most of the Dakotas' land. In the process, the treaties destroyed their ancient, semi-*nomadic* (traveling) way of life. Chiefs like Little Crow, who had signed the agreements in hopes of preventing more seizures of land and warfare with a distant "Great Father" (the U.S. president), felt cheated and powerless. In the early 1860s, fresh problems arose for the Indians. Game was scarce. Crops had failed because of drought. As Congress argued whether to give the Indians their treaty annuities in cash or gold, no money at all reached the reservations. Traders refused to release food to the Indians without payment. Unrest grew. Extremists suggested that there was no *famine* (hunger), that the complaints were a setup for an attack on the Union orchestrated by clever *secessionists* (Americans who didn't want to belong to the Union).

Meanwhile, conflict was brewing between the so-called "blanket" Dakota Indians, who clung to their traditional ways, and the "cut-hairs," who adopted white customs, including cropped hair, and settled down to farm like their white neighbors. A rift was also growing between Dakota elders, who warned against violence as overwhelming numbers of whites moved westward, and young Indian warriors, who organized themselves into Soldier Lodges and made plans to regain traditional *prestige* (honor) through the arts of warfare.

In one sense, these warriors and the would-be soldiers at Fort Snelling had much in common. But there was one major difference: tactics. The Union Army marched and fought in orderly ranks while the Dakota relied on hiding and ambush. Another difference was evident in each side's attitude toward death. The Dakota went to war for glory, to kill the enemy and to bring back evidence that they had done so. The white man often seemed to find the greatest glory in dying for a cause. But the whites had the printing presses—the means to publicly present the coming conflict as an unequal battle between bloodthirsty savages and peaceful settlers. Minnesotans would build the monuments and write the histories in language that demonized the enemy for striking precisely when the Civil War had left Minnesota weak and defenseless.

In the summer of 1862, Minnesota's two-front war began in Acton Township in western Meeker County. There, on the hot morning of August 17, four young Dakota men, hungry and discouraged from a failed hunting trip, came upon a nestful of eggs. One of the men was determined to eat the eggs on the spot but the rest refused, fearful of reprisals from Robinson Jones, a local farmer. A quarrel broke out. Amid charges of cowardice, the eggs were broken and the group went to the farmhouse to demand liquor instead. Although denied "firewater," they and Jones went off to the nearby Howard Baker homestead, where a target-shooting match began. When Jones and Baker had taken their turns and emptied their guns, the Indians suddenly turned on their hosts and killed five people, including Jones's wife. Two surviving women spread the alarm as the Indians fled to the Lower Agency on

A 1909 sketch shows the August 1862 Acton attack.

stolen horses. The U.S.–Dakota War of 1862, also known as the Great Sioux Uprising, had begun.

The U.S.–Dakota War

By the time the uprising was over, untold thousands of Dakota had been hanged, killed in battle, shot for bounty money, or shipped into exile. Cries for vengeance were heard as far away as Washington, D.C. Tales of torture and mutilation gripped the national imagination. Forty thousand terrified Minnesotans had fled their homes in fear; many would never return.

Although the killings at Acton may have ignited the bloodshed, the underlying causes were more subtle. As far back as the treaties of the 1850s, Little Crow and other Indians who signed the documents felt that turning over their ancestral lands to the white man spelled doom for the Dakota. In 1861 and 1862, his misgivings were confirmed by severe food shortages. His people gathered around the warehouses at the agencies, demanding provisions before their long-delayed annuities arrived from Washington. Some traders doled out a little flour, but by June 1862 most of them had cut off the Indians' credit. The starving

Indians had no choice but to kill and eat their own dogs and horses.

As the misery grew, one trader was heard to say, "If they are hungry, let them eat grass and their own *dung* (feces)." Such statements only made the situation more *volatile* (unstable). On August 18, the Dakota attacked the Lower Agency in force. They killed Myron Myrick (he was found with his mouth stuffed with grass) and destroyed white property in the vicinity. Victims were axed, beheaded, and disemboweled by warriors charged with desperate emotion and, sometimes, with liquor. The attacks seemed random: one family lived, another died horribly. But while many of the Dakota elders rejected warfare against whites, the Soldier Lodges had found a reluctant leader in Little Crow. When first approached by the young hotheads, he argued against their plan. "You will die like rabbits when hungry wolves hunt them," he said. The enemy's superior numbers and fearsome weaponry would quickly overwhelm the Indians. When accused of timidity, however, Little Crow relented. "Little Crow is not a coward," he declared. "He will die with you."

The refugees of the Redwood Agency attack made their way to Fort Ridgely, thirteen miles to the east. Located at the head of navigation on the Minnesota River, Fort Ridgely was intended to be a major supply point for federal troops. Because of the Civil War, however, the frontier forts of Minnesota were shorthanded and vulnerable. (Fort Snelling itself had been sold in the 1850s and was being lent back to Uncle Sam by its owner for military training.) Troops sent out from Fort Ridgely to control the situation were ambushed at Redwood Ferry. By the time the encounter was over, only twenty-two soldiers were left at the fort to protect more than 250 frightened exiles from the countryside. On August 20 and 22, Little Crow's army of 800 braves circled the fort, certain of victory, only to be driven off by artillery volleys. Later, Chief Big Eagle would say that Fort Ridgely had been the door to the Minnesota Valley and even to St. Paul

The Carrothers children were taken captive by the Dakota in 1862 and later released. Tintype, ca. 1872.

itself. Had he and his men captured the fort, the history of the state might have been remarkably different. But the door remained closed and the Indian army headed instead to New Ulm, Hutchinson, Forest City, and a host of smaller frontier towns.

The defense of New Ulm by its German settlers and soldiers from St. Peter under the command of Judge Charles Flandrau was one of the most stirring episodes of the war, according to the state's newspapers, which were whipped into a frenzy of their own by stories from victims of the conflict. Abolitionist Jane Grey Swisshelm was one of many newspaper editors calling for the swift extermination of the Indians. Under the pressure of the emergency, Governor Ramsey persuaded his old friend Henry Sibley to head upriver with volunteers to end the violence. Meanwhile, he asked for quick action from Washington, D.C., telling Lincoln by wire that "this is not our war; it is a national war." Sibley was

Henry Sibley poses in the uniform he wore to put down the Dakota uprising in 1862.

Refugees fleeing Indian attacks on the Minnesota prairie. The photo was taken by one of this group on August 21, 1862. Some frightened settlers fled to New Ulm and others to Mankato. Hostile Indians later attacked New Ulm.

German immigrant artist Anton Gág re-created the Dakota attack on New Ulm in a 1904 painting.

often criticized for the slow, deliberate pace of his march to the northwest. Jane Swisshelm was one of his most virulent detractors. But he moved cautiously because he lacked supplies and was uncertain about when and whether *veteran* (experienced) federal troops of the Third Minnesota would arrive in numbers.

A Minnesota Tragedy

The U.S.–Dakota War ended in late September 1862 at Camp Release, near present-day Montevideo, where 269 prisoners of the Dakota were handed over. By that time, many of the warriors had fled to the Dakota Territory or Canada. Hundreds of those who remained behind were put on trial on the spot. The rest were transported to a kind of prison camp outside Fort Snelling while officials decided what to do with them. Sibley's military court tried up to forty men a day. By early November, 392 Indians had been charged, 307 sentenced to death, and 16 given lengthy prison terms. While many missionaries, including Bishop Whipple, pleaded for the prisoners' lives, the public cried out for vengeance. As Abraham

Lincoln pondered the question, Governor Ramsey told him, "Nothing but the speedy execution of the tried and convicted Sioux will save us from scenes of outrage."

Already, troops moving the condemned Indians southward had been attacked several times by mobs of angry civilians. A wagon train of Dakota women and children was stormed in Hutchinson, where a nursing baby was snatched from its mother and killed, and again in New Ulm, where victims of the conflict were being reburied as the Indians were driven through town. When his final decision was announced, President Lincoln was *pilloried* (criticized) for condemning only thirty-nine prisoners, a number later reduced to thirty-eight. On December 26, 1862, as thousands cheered, those men were publicly hanged from a single scaffold in Mankato in the largest mass execution in American history. The bodies were hastily buried on a sandbar in a shallow mass grave. (Dr. William Worrall Mayo dug up the corpse of Cut Nose and used it to instruct his sons, Charles H. and William J., in the finer points of anatomy; the brothers later founded the Mayo Clinic.) The 1,700 Indians confined at Fort Snelling endured a kind of living death. Tourists gaped at them. Exposure

The women of New Ulm attacked Dakota captives being driven through their town.

Episcopal bishop Henry Whipple baptized forty-seven Dakota prisoners at Fort Snelling in 1863.

Bounty payment of $500 paid to Nathan Lamson for the killing of Little Crow.

to cold and an outbreak of measles killed many. Of those herded into the encampment, only 250 remained to make the long journey into permanent exile on the Missouri River, far from Minnesota.

Some of the Dakota tried to return to Minnesota. Little Crow and nineteen of his loyal followers came back in 1863. On the morning of July 3, he and his young son were picking wild raspberries in a field near Hutchinson. Nathan Lamson and his son saw them, opened fire, and killed Little Crow. The chief's son laid out fresh moccasins for his father's trip to the spirit world, gave him a drink of water, and crept quietly away. Lamson got a $500 bounty check from the state. Little Crow's body was brought into Hutchinson, where he was scalped; boys put Fourth of July firecrackers in his ears and nose. The corpse was dumped in a garbage pit.

The U.S.–Dakota War was over.

Little Crow in 1851, painted by Frank Blackwell Mayer, 1895.

veterans of the civil war

WHEN THE CIVIL WAR ended in 1865 and Minnesota's soldiers came back to St. Paul, there was some grumbling in the ranks. The First Minnesota had been greeted the year before with cheers, honors, and parades. The Fourth Minnesota, however, passed through the city with little fanfare. But the situation was swiftly remedied. A welcoming committee set up triumphal arches of pine branches, held banquets marked with speeches of gratitude, and tried to answer the question posed by a chaplain of the Seventh Regiment. How, he wondered, would his charges get on in civilian life: Would the state forever

Grand Army of the Republic medals were issued to veterans at their periodic reunions.

The last four surviving Civil War veterans of Stillwater's "Last Man's Club", about 1920. Members of the First Minnesota Volunteer Infantry Regiment, the veterans met yearly, draping their deceased comrades' empty chairs in black. To the last survivor would belong the bottle of wine in the rosewood cask pictured with the men. The last man would be Captain Charles M. Lockwood on the right, a grain merchant and government agent, who died in 1925. When the cask was finally opened in 1927, the wine had turned to vinegar.

regard them as returning "heroes and saviors of their country"—or would they soon be forgotten amid the prosperity of peacetime?

In fact, many Civil War veterans took advantage of the Homestead Act (passed in 1862) and their army pensions to buy land and improve their farmsteads. By the time they reached middle age, they had begun to flex their political muscle through the heavily Republican Grand Army of the Republic. It was the influence of organized veterans that created the Minnesota Soldiers' Home in Minneapolis in 1887. Eight veterans served as governors of the state between 1863 and 1905, beginning with Stephen Miller and ending with Samuel Van Sant. Major battles of the war were re-created in *panoramas* (massive oil paintings on canvas) attracting more than 100,000 spectators around the nation in

1886 alone. At the State Fair grandstand for two generations, mock Civil War battles—some of them using veterans as actors—lit up the night with bursts of artificial artillery.

The last surviving veteran of the Union Army was Albert Woolson, who lived in Duluth. He died in 1956 at the age of 109, although new data suggests that he may actually have been three years younger. In 1949, Woolson was one of only six veterans who attended the final national encampment of the Grand Army of the Republic in Indianapolis. His view of the Civil War? "We were fighting our brothers. In that there was no glory."

minnesota's trophy

ON THE THIRD AND FINAL DAY of the bloody Battle of Gettysburg, Marshall Sherman of First Minnesota's C Company captured the battle flag of the 28th Virginia Volunteer Infantry. For his bravery, Private Sherman, who was from St. Paul, was later awarded the Congressional Medal of Honor.

In the 1990s, a group of Civil War reenactors in Roanoke, Virginia, asked the Minnesota Historical Society to return the captured flag. For six long years, Virginia and Minnesota engaged in a quiet tug-of-war over custody of the banner. Governors, senators, generals, and Jesse Jackson's congressman-son all gave their opinions on the issue. But for many Minnesotans, the question was whether the captured flag should go back to a state that still paid *homage* (respect) to the Confederate history of slavery. African Americans in Minnesota and elsewhere thought it should stay where it was, in the possession of those whose ancestors had fought on the Union side to free the slaves. Minnesota governor Jesse Ventura put the matter in the clearest possible terms in 2001: "How many Minnesota boys spilled their guts and blood on that same battlefield?" he asked. "We won the flag."

By the third day of the Battle of Gettysburg, the First Minnesota Volunteers had been decimated, with 215 of its 262 troops killed or wounded. Ventura considered the battleflag a hard-won prize of war. "Tell them [Virginia] to come and get it," he said. "That's ours—it's not a POW." Historians and the curators later agreed with the governor. The flag remains in Minnesota.

Minnesotans captured the flag of the 28th Virginia at Gettysburg.

James R. Meeker's 1877 painting of a wheat farm at Lake Pepin.

chapter five

WHEAT, TIMBER, FLOUR, IRON

AFTER THE CIVIL WAR, Minnesota enjoyed rapid growth and widespread prosperity. The 1865 census saw a gain of more than 250,000 people in five years. The war itself created demand for crops and lumber while the absence of working men in their prime led to increased *mechanization* (machinery substituted for manpower) across a broad section of what is now called the Middle West. And the war had demonstrated the need for more and better rail transportation. In 1869, thanks to land grants from the government, the first transcontinental railroad was completed on the southern route, near Ogden, Utah. Soon, a northern route would open the natural resources of Minnesota to trade with the Atlantic and the Pacific Coasts and beyond.

Postwar Industry

Although Indian wars in the West continued off and on for a generation, the removal of the Dakota opened huge new tracts of Minnesota prairie for planting and harvesting wheat. Pioneers had planted plots of wheat in the 1850s. Several small grist-mills on the Mississippi at St. Anthony Falls ground coarse flour for local use. But wheat crops often failed from attacks by fungus or insects. Wheat also

rapidly depleted the soil of nutrients, which was another drawback. Despite these disadvantages and the interruption of the Dakota War, however, the 1863 wheat harvest reached 5 million bushels. By the boom year of 1865, the total was more than 9

A wagonload of wheat heads to the mill, ca. 1900.

million. Farming as a means to feed one's family was becoming farming as a major industry. Modern agriculture began in the fertile soil of southern and western Minnesota.

This cumbersome steam engine was used to thresh wheat, ca. 1910.

Harvesting wheat the old-fashioned way on the Oliver H. Kelley Farm, a Minnesota Historical Society site in Elk River.

Minnesota wheat might never have become an important product in the global marketplace, however, had it not been for the forests: the Big Woods between the Mississippi and the St. Croix and the seemingly endless stands of pine beyond. As early as 1837, Henry Sibley and his partners had negotiated with the Ojibwe to cut hardwoods along the St. Croix and Snake Rivers. To ship wood products to wider markets, however, required not only streams to float the logs out of the woods but sawmills to transform rough timber into boards and window frames. During the early 1860s, the C. C. Washburn family and their associates opened a lumber mill at St. Anthony Falls. The Washburns became early leaders in the creation of the Minneapolis flour milling industry because they already knew how to power machinery with water. By 1865, the area was a hive of new businesses, as barrelmakers, sash and door factories, and machine shops grew up to serve the mills.

The Hunger for Lumber

The demand for lumber was huge. Entire houses were shipped out from Minneapolis in railroad cars. Boards, doors, windows, and trim came packaged and ready to build over precut frames. A two-room cabin, suitable for a homesteader, cost $75. Omaha, Kansas City, St. Louis, Topeka, and Des Moines—the cities of the grassland states and territories—all were constructed of Minnesota white pine from virgin forests where the trees grew straight as arrows, more than 200 feet tall and 6 feet across the trunk. Predicted one prophet of the day, "Seventy mills in seventy years couldn't exhaust the white pine I have seen." Sadly, he was wrong. The forests disappeared all too quickly. In that era, conservation was less important than the needs of an expanding population.

Paul Bunyan was a mythical lumberjack whose footsteps were so mammoth that they, along with those of his blue ox, Babe, created Minnesota's 10,000 lakes. This statue was built in Bemidji, ca. 1938.

the seventeenth century. Wood became an increasingly valuable commodity as immigrant farmers from Europe began to build homes and barns across the Midwest, spurred on by the 160 acres promised to each new settler by the Homestead Act.

The Homestead Act itself sparked abuses within the lumber industry. Some loggers filed false claims on behalf of farmers and then cut down all the trees on a property. When Minnesota appointed a commissioner to issue cutting permits for public lands that were acquired through auction, critics charged that the permits often went to the commissioner's *cronies* (friends) at low prices. *Bribery* (money for favors) was common. So was outright thievery of standing trees. By 1905, when more than 2 billion board feet of Minnesota lumber were harvested, the state's forests had been stripped bare of their finest trees. The timber cruisers moved on to Washington and Oregon. Minnesota witnessed its last log drive—a huge raft of pine logs floated down from the north woods—in 1937 on the Little Big Fork River.

Red River Lumber Company advertising booklet, 1914.

Timber "cruisers" employed by lumbermen like Frederick Weyerhaeuser were sent out to estimate the quality and quantity of sections of forest. They also planned locations for lumber camps and the roads on which to slide the cut timber to a nearby stream. Crews followed with steam-powered equipment and factory-like methods of cutting, shaping, and moving the product. Timber was scarce in the East, where trees had been cut to create farmland since

As early as 1876, according to one historian of the industry, enough lumber had been cut in Minnesota to circle the

Two-person "timberhog" chainsaw used in Minnesota in the 1940s.

Minnesota lumberjacks in camp, ca. 1885. Notice that the man in the front row, second from right, and others are wearing their pants in a cut-off high-water fashion. This helped prevent snagging their trouser legs on their spiked boots and other obstacles.

earth one-and-a-half times with a one-foot-wide band of finished boards.

The World's Best Flour

The same waterpower that ran the machinery for cutting and planing lumber would also provide the energy that would make Minneapolis—known as "Sawdust Town"—into the world's greatest flour producer. Between 1880 and 1930, housewives from Minnesota to Minsk baked their bread with top-of-the-line wheat flours from the "Mill City" on the Mississippi. Washburn-Crosby's Gold Medal brand flour is still on supermarket shelves today, along with Pillsbury's Best. The remarkable growth in production—in the 1920s, the Washburn Mill still produced a million pounds of flour every day—turned Minneapolis from a sleepy town into one of the nation's most important business centers. That growth was the result of several forces. First, the timber industry had proven the capacity of St. Anthony Falls to run machinery for grinding wheat. Second, farmers grew more wheat because they could sell it readily to the mills. Third, new rail lines helped to bring farmers to the land, wheat to the mills, and flour to distant destinations. And finally, a milling technology had been invented that was specially suited to the tough-shelled red spring wheat that grew best in Minnesota.

The grindstones that were used to mill the softer winter wheat grown elsewhere didn't work well with Minnesota's harder spring wheat. The stones crushed the shell but left bits of bran behind, which gave the flour a dingy color. The stones also crushed the wheat kernel, which released oil into the flour and caused it to spoil quickly. But when spring wheat was crushed between metal or porcelain rollers and then blasted with air, the result was a pure white flour with greater nutritional value. The process increased the yield per bushel too. After Washburn's premium flour won the gold medal at a prestigious millers' competition in Cincinnati in 1878, Minnesota became known as the flour capital of the world. The Minneapolis Chamber of Commerce patted the city on the back in 1884 by saying, "The flour mills of Minneapolis, and their superior products, have given our city a world wide name and most enviable reputation!"

The demands of industry left their ugly mark on the falls. The limestone ledge over which the water spilled was chipped away by tumbling logs. Tunnels built to harness the flow of water to the mills collapsed. As early as 1857 a visitor had observed that "all the machinery of the world almost must be driven in the space of [a] mile of darkling water." The works of man had "marred God's beautiful workmanship." But scenery took a back seat when a great city was rising and the towns of the plains beyond it were bustling with energy. In Hastings, wrote a traveler, there was "wheat everywhere . . . wagon loads of wheat pouring down to the levee; wheat in the streets; wheat on the sidewalks." There was wheat, it seemed, everywhere one looked—west to the Dakotas, north to the Red River Valley, south to Iowa.

Wheat and Railroads

The increasing demand for wheat spawned "bonanza farms" covering thousands of acres of fertile land in the Red River Valley. Owners used gangs of hired workers and the best modern machinery—reapers, binders, plows, and steam threshers—to make

Oliver Dalrymple's gigantic farm in pioneer Dakota County made him the largest grower of wheat in the world.

millionaires out of their investors. Oliver Dalrymple, a St. Paul lawyer who eventually owned more than 100,000 acres, shipped 32,000 bushels of wheat to Minneapolis in 1876 alone. Smaller farms still accounted for the majority of the crop, but both kinds of agriculture relied on the railroad and the grain elevators along the tracks to deliver the wheat to market. In 1862, there were ten miles of track in Minnesota, running between St. Paul and St. Anthony (now part of Minneapolis). The first locomotive in the state, the *William Crooks*, was built in New Jersey, shipped by rail to La Crosse, Wisconsin, and transported up the Mississippi on the steamboat *Alhambra* in September 1861. During the Panic of 1873, St. Paul's Northern Pacific line, owned by financier Jay Cooke, went bankrupt. This second transcontinental route was later acquired by James J. Hill, nicknamed the "Empire Builder," who dominated Minnesota business throughout the 1880s and 1890s from his mansion on Summit Avenue in St. Paul. Construction of Hill's Great Northern Railroad brought hard-working Irish and Scandinavian immigrants to the state. They often laid two miles of track a day for $2, which were excellent wages for the time. But the farmers and millers benefited most from the railroad. Their whole grain and milled flour no longer had to make the long, slow trip to the Gulf of Mexico by boat. Now, as rail lines radiated toward Chicago, New York, and the markets of

away from the rivers that had once been Minnesota's lifelines. Where the trains went, so went the settlers. Railroad companies owned huge tracts of land along their routes; the government had granted them the land to encourage them to build the railway system. Farmers often bought their homesteads from the railroads.

The *William Crooks,* owned by James J. Hill, was Minnesota's first locomotive. Named for the chief mechanical engineer of the St. Paul & Pacific Railroad, the first railroad in Minnesota, the *William Crooks* carried the historic first trainload of passengers between St. Paul and St. Anthony (now part of Minneapolis) on June 28, 1862.

Asia and the Pacific, Minnesota became part of the global marketplace.

Because of the railroad, towns could thrive inland,

But the real return came when farms began to produce and paid the railroad to move their crops to market. Meanwhile, the railroad shipped the necessities of life back to the countryside: ready-made houses, machinery, furniture, and clothes. The relationship between land, farmers, railroads, and the state was indeed complex.

Railroads, as they pushed westward, also shaped the

"Empire Builder" James J. Hill's Great Northern Railroad would reach the West Coast in 1893. Mr. Hill attributed his enormous success to: "work, hard work, intelligent work, and then more work."

When James J. Hill died in his Summit Avenue home on May 29, 1916, after amassing a fortune estimated at $63 million, he was one of the wealthiest and most powerful men in America.

landscape of rural Minnesota. Towns followed the tracks, each one roughly six miles from its neighbor. Business executives in St. Paul calculated that a farmer with a wagonload of wheat could go just about three miles into town and three miles back again in a single day. The towns of western Minnesota tended to be laid out according to similar plans, also plotted by the railroad. Positions closest to the tracks went to the train depot, grain storage elevators, and stockyards. Stores, schools, and civic buildings tended to cluster nearby. The "wrong side of the tracks" harbored the more disreputable features of small town life, including the saloon. Older towns that were bypassed by the trains, like Mantorville, gradually withered away. But new cities sprang to life too. In 1869, Duluth had only fourteen crude buildings when financier Jay Cooke built that city's first grain elevator. A year earlier, as legend has it, Cooke paddled a canoe out into Lake Superior to survey the place, wearing a top hat, cloth shoes, a colored waistcoat, a gold watch chain, and a fancy cane. By 1870, linked to St. Paul and Chicago by railroad, Duluth began its rise to prominence as one of the nation's great inland ports.

Minnesotans from Europe

Because the railroads needed customers—because progress was measured in Minnesota's appeal to newcomers—both the rail lines and the state eagerly recruited immigrants in Europe. Colonel Hans Mattson, a Swede from Vasa who had fought for Minnesota in the Civil War and later served as a land agent for the St. Paul & Pacific Railroad, was appointed commissioner of a State Board of Immigration in 1867. In 1868, he traveled to Sweden to recruit his former countrymen to farm in Minnesota's wheatlands. Minnesota even set up a special office in Canada to guide newly arrived Norwegians straight to Minneapolis from Quebec. Mattson's descriptions of the land of milk and honey that awaited them were poetic and sometimes fictional. Like other state boosters, he claimed that the brisk climate of the prairies made Minnesota a refuge for invalids.

Railroad titan James J. Hill, as well as the state government, distributed immigrant pamphlets in German and Scandinavian languages, painting a picture of paradise on the plains. "The whole surface of the state is literally begemmed with innumerable lakes," read one breathless passage. "Their picturesque beauty and loveliness, with their pebbly bottoms, transparent waters, wooded shores and sylvan associations, must be seen to be fully appreciated." Other promotional literature showed pictures of strings of fish, numbering in the hundreds, said to be caught in a single morning at one of these lakes.

Some of the most moving and beautiful descriptions of Minnesota come in novels about the immigrant experience. Norwegian Knute Hamsun, who worked on the bonanza farm owned by Oliver Dalrymple in 1887 and who won the Nobel Prize for literature in 1920, remembered the grass and wheat of the prairie as "golden green and endless as the sea." Other Scandinavians, like O. E. Rolvaag, described characters traveling by covered wagon as frightened by the loneliness of the flat landscape, a "plain so wide that the rim of the heavens cut down on it around the entire horizon." Beret, the heroine of Rolvaag's *Giants in the Earth*, compares the landscape of southern Minnesota to the boundless sea she has just crossed; she longs for a tree, a fixed point, a place to hide from the rippling emptiness. Karl Oskar and Kristina, the Swedish newcomers in Vilhelm Moberg's *Unto a Good Land*, find friendlier surroundings in the woodlands above the Twin Cities, but Kristina fears her restless husband will soon want to press on into the unknown lands to their west.

But the best recommendation of all, according to those immigrants who came to live in Minnesota, were the "America letters" sent home by earlier settlers, describing how they had prospered in the state.

By the 1870s, almost 40 percent of the state's population was from another country. One Minnesotan described the Germans, the Norwegians, the Swedes, and the Irish who answered the call of the Immigration Board as "the most virile, industrious, and moral of foreigners." Not everybody prospered, of course—at least not all of the time. Oliver Kelley, who had filed a claim on a piece of land near Elk River, went on to found the National Grange of the Patrons of Husbandry (also known as the Grangers) in 1867. Throughout the 1870s, this union for farmers fought for laws that would guarantee reasonable freight rates for shipping their grain to market. They were often successful at passing such laws, but the railroads ignored them. This was the heyday of the "robber baron," who always had the advantage against a non-English-speaking farmer homesteading 160 acres of land in the middle of nowhere and without resources or influence. Under the iron law of nineteenth-century economics, the rich got richer, usually at the expense of the poor.

An Industrial Accident

Progress sometimes came at a price. At 6:00 p.m. on May 2, 1878, the Washburn "A" Mill in Minneapolis exploded. Its six-foot-thick walls of stone toppled two other mills nearby. In an instant, the Mill City lost a third of its capacity to turn wheat into premium flour. The blast broke windows for miles around and sent giant waves down the mighty Mississippi as far as St. Paul. Eighteen plant workers were killed; they were honored in a public funeral. The cause of the explosion was found to be the 3,000 pounds of dust generated every day by the milling process. The disaster led to improvements in the equipment for filtering explosive particles from the air. The mills grew larger. The railroads carried ever more barrels of flour. The farmers planted more and more spring wheat.

Mountains of Iron

In northeastern Minnesota, timber cruisers looking for the last stands of white pine literally stumbled across the nation's greatest deposits of iron ore: the Vermilion, the Mesabi, and the Cuyuna iron ranges. At first, nobody knew what to make of the mineral ores lying right beneath their feet. Proper iron ore, they believed, was always hidden in seams running deep underground. The first "rush" to the area came in the 1860s, just after the Civil War, by prospectors looking for gold nuggets. The Vermilion Lake gold rush may have been a hoax, but it stirred interest in the use of the odd, reddish deposits that seemed to be everywhere. Minnesota iron was displayed at the great Paris Exposition of 1867 and at the Smithsonian Institution in Washington, D.C. But it was only in the 1880s and 1890s that surface mining began in earnest in Minnesota mining towns like

Interior view of Washburn "A" Mill, Minneapolis.

Washburn "A" Mill, ca. 1875, before an explosion destroyed it.

Tower, Mountain Iron, and Virginia. Great steam-powered shovels were used to remove the soft hematite ore. High taxes on that ore helped build lavish civic buildings on "the Range," like the richly decorated high school at Hibbing. The iron rush also built the huge ore docks at Duluth, Superior, and Two Harbors. That iron fed the furnaces that made the rails that brought the wheat to the mills. And so it went, in a seemingly endless circle of extraction, manufacturing, and agriculture. The unique combination of natural resources and the means of exploiting them made Minnesota a major economic force as the nineteenth century drew to a close.

Two years after the Merritt brothers discovered iron ore in the area, the town of Biwabik (which means "valuable" in the Ojibwe language) shipped its first ore to Lake Superior. Biwabik's population soared to 3,000 as miners poured in from Finland, Norway, Sweden, Italy, and the Austro-Hungarian Empire to work in the seven mines that were dug within the city limits.

The Tower-Soudan mine, pictured here in 1890, is the oldest and deepest iron mine in Minnesota. Tourists visiting the mine today can don hard hats and descend in a "cage" a half mile down into the earth. There they board a train for a three-quarter-mile trip to the last and deepest area mined.

grasshoppers!

DESPITE MINNESOTA'S PROSPEROUS times after the Civil War, the state had more than its share of troubles. There was the Northfield bank robbery staged by Jesse James and his gang in 1876; the so-called "long winter" of 1880–1881, described in Laura Ingalls Wilder's book of the same name; and the national Panic of 1873, which threw financial markets into a tailspin. But the worst of all these trials was the grasshopper plague of 1873–1877.

It came in late spring, on the heels of a terrible January blizzard. Just as things were getting back to normal, disaster struck. Around noon on the beautiful, sunny afternoon of June 12, 1873, remembered one victim, "the sky was darkened by myriads of grasshoppers and no green thing could be seen." The gardens were eaten first, then the wheat. The fields looked as if they had been burned. When all that was gone, the 'hoppers ate the coats and pants right off the clothesline—and then devoured the clothesline! Crops in thirteen counties in southwestern Minnesota were devastated.

As wheat production fell to half of its normal harvest in the affected areas, the mills in Minneapolis felt the pinch. Volunteer committees in the cities collected aid pledges. But state and federal governments had little experience in coping with crises other than war. Their philosophy was one of *laissez-faire*, or letting things work themselves out. Minnesota's Episcopal bishop, Henry Whipple, called for state aid, convinced the grasshoppers were a scourge sent by God as *retribution* (payment) for the loose morals some people showed after the Civil War. Minnesota governor John Pillsbury organized a multistate grasshopper commission, which met in Omaha, Nebraska, in 1876, as the insects continued to swarm. The commission failed to scare off the grasshoppers.

Farmers built special plows with long strips of iron or cloth dipped in sticky molasses to drag the grasshoppers out of the fields. *Bounties* (rewards) were offered on live 'hoppers: a dollar per bushel or 50 cents a gallon for their eggs. There was a grasshopper draft in some counties. Able-bodied men between ages twenty-one and sixty were expected to spend one day a week battling the insects. If they didn't, they had to pay a dollar for every day of work they missed. When all else failed,

Farmers were no match for the grasshopper plague in Minnesota.

Governor Pillsbury declared a statewide day of prayer and fasting for deliverance on April 26, 1877.

The grasshoppers disappeared as suddenly as they had arrived. Unexpectedly, on July 1, 1877, the grasshoppers (actually, they were a species of Rocky Mountain locust) took flight and sailed out of Minnesota. Their *exodus* (mass exit) was followed by a miraculous crop of wheat, more than 30 million bushels.

the stone arch bridge

THE STONE ARCH BRIDGE spanning the Mississippi just below the Falls of St. Anthony is the greatest surviving monument to 1880s Minnesota. Built by James J. Hill between 1882 and 1883, it carried his Great Northern railcars into the heart of the flour mill district of Minneapolis. The bridge had twenty-three graceful arches and curved across the stream in a long, archlike form of its own. The railroad connection put the young city of Minneapolis on the map, and it stamped Hill as one of America's major captains of industry.

The bridge served several purposes. It brought Hill's St. Paul, Minneapolis, & Manitoba Railroad (later known as the Great Northern) into the heart of Minneapolis. The bridge *funneled* (directed) flour to the vast markets reached by the fast-growing network of tracks. It also transported passengers to the new train depot on the west bank of the river, at the intersection of Hennepin and Nicollet.

As the bridge was being built, it was known as "Hill's Folly" for its cost—$650,000, a fortune in that day—and its design. Hill could have built a cheaper, straighter bridge above the falls, but he had been warned that construction could destroy the great waterpower resource forever. The cost was further increased by the use of the strongest stone blocks then available: local Platteville limestone, St. Cloud granite, and a special magnesium limestone quarried in Stone City, Iowa. The curve of the bridge, with its massive abutments that supported the arches, helped to deflect floating debris. But the curve also added drama and symbolic weight to a piece of clever engineering.

One hundred and twenty-five years later, the bridge resonates with power and force of will. Although it is now a pleasure park and a tourist attraction, the structure is still the anchor that ties Minneapolis to its river and to its history.

The Stone Arch bridge leading to the Minneapolis milling district.

This splendiferous float in the gigantic parade that celebrated the completion of James J. Hill's
Great Northern Railroad to the West Coast in 1893 touted St. Paul as "the center of North America."

chapter six

CELEBRATING COMPETING DEFINING

IT IS EASY TO DISMISS Minnesota's annual round of public entertainments as just that: entertainment. There are dozens of them: the St. Paul Winter Carnival, the Minneapolis Aquatennial, the Taste of Minnesota, the Edina Art Fair, the Mora Vasaloppet (a cross-country ski race), and many Mexican, Swedish, Irish, and German festivals, as well as the Land of the Loon Festival, Voyageur Days, Muskie Days, Bullhead Days, and the Paul Bunyan Winter Carnival. All of them offer fried food aplenty, craft booths, music, and local characters on parade. But there is more to organized celebrations than that.

In the 1880s and 1890s, festivals were serious business. When they first came into their own, they did so on a grand scale that staggers the modern imagination. Indeed, festivals were often lavishly funded by businesses or paid tribute to them. The nature of a particular event—what the orators said, where the people gathered, what kinds of symbolic decorations were in place, what Minnesotans came to see and share at the festivals—often reveals a complicated set of goals. The public galas of the late nineteenth century celebrated Minnesota's accomplishments and defined the state's role in the affairs of the region and the

nation at large. They also provided occasions for competition—farmer against farmer, firm against firm, city against city, Minnesota against the world.

Celebrating the Railroad

The year 1883 marked the beginning of a furious round of festivals in St. Paul and its so-called suburb (Minneapolis!), all centered on the railroad. The year in which the Stone Arch Bridge was completed, bringing traffic into the heart of Minneapolis, was also the year in which the Northern Pacific opened a transcontinental line to the Pacific. The timing couldn't have been better. The previous year, 1882, had seen its share of troubles. Flooding in the upper and lower valleys of the Mississippi had left 85,000 Minnesotans homeless. But despite the hardships, the economy was booming. Now was the time to rejoice. Elsewhere, elaborate "golden spike" rituals that celebrated the connection of segments of the ever-expanding American railroad system were old news. In the "New Northwest," however, a pending link between Minnesota and China from rail to boat generated much excitement. A gigantic gala was planned in St. Paul to greet Henry Villard, president of the Northern Pacific, and his five hundred guests as they passed through town on September 3 on an official inspection trip to the railhead at Tacoma, Washington.

Photographs show visitors and their hosts parading through triumphal arches that were several stories high at the major intersections of downtown St. Paul. Keyhole arches, Egyptian arches, pictorial arches (one showed the *William Crooks,* Minnesota's first railroad engine)—even an arch constructed by the Kelly, Allen & Moon Mercantile establishment out of barrels and crates of groceries—decorated the parade route. Garlands of *bunting* (draped cloth) hung from nearby buildings. One hundred thousand little pennants bearing the initials "N.P.R." fluttered from every surface. A stereograph card of the somewhat more subdued festivities in Minneapolis reveals large landscape views hung across storefronts along with mottos, flags, and evergreens. The text printed along the edge of the scene says that the afternoon's celebration was attended "by no less than 100,000 people, among the distinguished being President Chester Arthur, Gen. U. S. Grant, Gen. Phillip Sheridan and others." In most reports describing well-attended events of the period, "100,000" seems to have meant "quite a few," whatever the real head count might have been.

Built of barrels and crates, this triumphal arch celebrated the completion of Henry Villard's Northern Pacific Railroad to Tacoma, Washington, in 1883. Villard also supported Thomas Edison's early ventures and in 1889 helped establish the Edison General Electric Company.

An arch at East Fourth and Rosabel, St. Paul, shows the locomotive *William Crooks* during the Northern Pacific celebration of 1883.

Competing "Twin Cities"

The real focus of attention in 1883 was the city of St. Paul, which ranked among the ten top commercial, financial, and transportation centers in the country. Although Minneapolitans ended September 3 with a huge bonfire kindled by thousands of railroad bonds bought over the years and now emphatically redeemed, the Northern Pacific celebration set off a bitter rivalry between the "twin cities" of Minneapolis and St. Paul. On September 10, 1884, Minneapolis businessmen held their own railroad gala—a testimonial dinner in honor of James J. Hill at which they presented him with a solid silver tray of outrageous size. The tray was engraved with an image of his

Minneapolis businessmen presented this commemorative tray by Tiffany to James J. Hill upon the completion of his Stone Arch Bridge.

CELEBRATING, COMPETING, DEFINING   **101**

Stone Arch Bridge surrounded by eight vignettes showing the story of his rise from obscurity to greatness. If the weight of the gift was any indication, Minneapolis was ready to do battle with St. Paul.

The competition actually began in the 1870s over which city should be the permanent host of the State Fair. The annual fair was the largest single gathering of Minnesotans. It had been held even before statehood was achieved, and it was crucial to defining just what Minnesota was. Crops and animals were judged. Gigantic cabbages and squash often took ribbons for sheer outlandishness, but they also demonstrated the richness of Minnesota soil to potential newcomers to the state. Women's work was honored in its own building. Without the handmade quilts, the home-churned butter, the rag carpets, the pies, and the preserves, many a pioneer family would not have survived their first winter. New agricultural machinery—much of it manufactured in Minnesota—was lined up, ready for try-outs and sales. Politicians gave speeches. Horses raced, some of them carrying daring ladies on their backs. Barkers sold gadgets that every home needed. Thanks to shows and exhibits of all kinds, fairgoers got a glimpse of a wide world beyond the borders of a single state. Why, back in 1857, at the Third Territorial Fair held on St. Paul's Capitol Square, a man named William Marko—"The Great Marco"—ascended to the heavens in a basket dangling beneath a giant balloon and floated gently away. He and his

The first official Minnesota State Fair was held in 1859, the year after Minnesota was granted statehood.

balloon were later found at Lake Phalen, or was it Forest Lake?

A Home for the State Fair

For many years, beginning in 1864, Minnesota's State Fair was a kind of "circus wagon" event, traveling from town to town—any place that agreed to put up the necessary buildings and donate prizes. Not surprisingly, most of these early fairgrounds were in the southern part of the state, in wheat country. But even during the years when the fair was setting up its livestock pens and reaper displays in Red Wing, Rochester, Winona, and Owatonna, it tended to gravitate more frequently toward St. Paul or Minneapolis. These were the largest cities in

Minnesota, made much more accessible by train. They were also great marketplaces to which country folk found themselves drawn anyway, in search of supplies, services, and a little entertainment.

Irritated that St. Paul seemed to host more than its share of state fairs, a Minneapolis booster and stockraiser organized a series of rival fairs in Minneapolis, beginning in 1871. Bill King's fairs relied more on industrial products than produce. His displays of bricks, safes, carriages, and heaps of iron ore gave his gatherings the characteristics of an urban trade show. Some years, both fairs—King's and the official state version—prospered. More often than not, however, profits were slim for everybody. But the heated

This postcard image of the Horticulture Building bespeaks growing pride in the State Fair's architecturally pleasing structures, ca. 1905.

competition worried rural interests, which began to demand a compromise between the rival cities, and a permanent fairgrounds.

In 1885, the State Agricultural Society settled on a "midway" site, halfway between "Peerless Minne" (Minneapolis) and "The Saintly City" (St. Paul). The Minnesota State Fairgrounds are still in the Midway neighborhood of St. Paul, at the intersection of Como and Snelling Avenues. But the compromise was not good enough for Bill King and the Minneapolis business community. In 1885, they began construction of a gigantic structure overlooking the Mississippi in which to house a permanent display so eye-popping that it would reduce the State Fair to little more than a "horse and cabbage" show. The venture quickly raised $100,000 for a "temple of industry and art" on the site of the old Winslow House hotel near St. Anthony Falls. Crowned by a 240-foot tower (and the famous "Angel Gabriel" weathervane from the old hotel), the eight-acre space included oil paintings from Europe, 236 plaster casts of ancient statues from New York's Metropolitan Museum, cacti from the Southwest, Spaulding baseballs, Colt rifles, Columbia bicycles, Baker's chocolate, and several milling machines, all brightly illuminated by 1,500 electric lights. All for a mere 25 cents admission fee!

The Exposition's Rise and Fall

Senator Cushman Davis, who spoke at the Minneapolis Exposition's grand opening in August 1886, praised its potential benefits. The arts, for example, could soften the harsh edges of city life and relieve "the tedium of the home life [that] drags most wearifully upon the wife and daughter." The statues and paintings were *antidotes* (remedies) to the city's

pool halls and saloons. The products of industry could inspire students at the nearby University of Minnesota to something more important than mere scholarship. The Exposition could inspire them to "creation itself." To business. To a new society, soon to be born in "this spacious temple of utility." Whether or not they took the senator's words to heart, 338,000 customers paid to traipse through the Exposition Building during its thirty-six-day run. Or perhaps it was the prospect of seeing a bust of President Grover Cleveland carved in a giant cake of White Lily soap made in Minneapolis that brought them through the turnstiles in such numbers!

There were eight Minneapolis Expositions in all. Yet the State Fair chugged along, getting bigger and better every year. Meanwhile, the rival show upstream cast

Minneapolis city fathers raised $250,000 in private funds to build the Exposition Building on Prince Street between Bank Street and Central Avenue in 1886. During its brief heyday, it hosted the National Republican Convention, the only presidential nominating convention ever held in Minnesota before 2008.

The old Minneapolis City Hall between Hennepin and Nicollet Avenues decked out for "Exposition Week," 1886.

about for novelties to lure back the crowds. Minneapolis staged public weddings, pretty-baby contests, special Colored People's Days. The enterprise succeeded only in attracting swarms of pickpockets who preyed on *naive* (unsuspecting) guests from out of town. In 1892, the Exposition hosted the National Republican Convention. Delegates fled to the train depot a day early, however, complaining that for all its claims to culture and refinement, there was nothing to eat in Minneapolis, except for the beans that organizers baked in thirty fire pits outside the building. President Benjamin Harrison was nominated for a second term (he lost), but the exposition flopped.

Its board of directors seemed to think the 1893 World's Columbian Exposition in Chicago might somehow induce tourists to stop at the Minneapolis Exposition on the way. Some local newspapers even hinted at a scheme to build a replica of the Eiffel Tower in Minneapolis to divert traffic from Chicago. It never happened. Even though the State Fair closed down to allow Minnesotans to bring their competition entries to the giant Chicago Fair, no one came to the Minneapolis Exposition. The weather was bad. Crops had failed. But the truth was the exposition had failed. Acting together on the Midway, the Twin Cities were unbeatable. Set apart from the rest of Minnesota, "the Prairie Queen"—Minneapolis's nickname—was just another town.

The St. Paul Winter Carnival

St. Paul, the fastest-growing city in the United States, was not pleased with the upstart Minneapolis Exposition. Nor were St. Paul's civic leaders happy with a report in a New York newspaper that called St. Paul "another Siberia, unfit for human habitation in winter." (Summer lasts only one month in Siberia, a vast region in Russia.) So, in 1885, St. Paul invented its Winter Carnival. As the editor of the *St. Paul Dispatch* put it, "St. Paul needs to arouse herself and gird on her armor for the battle of progress."

Montreal was famed for its cold-weather festival, which featured a splendid castle built of ice blocks. But when a smallpox epidemic swept through the Canadian city that year, St. Paul decided to hire the architects who had worked for Montreal's festival. With ice harvested from the Mississippi they built a towering castle (it lasted until the February thaw!) and kicked off an elaborate celebration of winter early in 1886. Like civic festivals held in New Orleans,

The first St. Paul Winter Carnival was held in 1886 and has since become an annual celebration and emblem of civic pride.

St. Louis, and elsewhere in the late nineteenth century, St. Paul's Winter Carnival was, and still is, organized around a made-up mythology. During the carnival, the forces of summertime (King Vulcanus Rex and his band of rascally Vulcans) stormed the castle of Borealis, King of Winter, and banished cold weather for another year. Meanwhile, the crowds watched toboggan runs, parades, snow sports, blanket tossing, and Dakota Indians performing tribal dances and demonstrating the use of dogsleds.

Organizers were delighted to find they had not only made money, but had also attracted favorable notice from every corner of the nation. The Winter Carnival is still going strong, as is the Minneapolis Aquatennial, which, since 1940, has celebrated summer with a similar festival with make-believe royalty.

In the beginning, the Winter Carnival in particular was a defiant act of self-definition, challenging all comers to speak ill of St. Paul. Over time, Minnesota's festivals have become rituals of affirmation of interest primarily to local people. Towns that once thought that building a castle out of potatoes or shocks of grain would bring commercial riches and countrywide attention now settle for a good time and a taste of glorious homemade pie (at the Braham Pie Festival every August, for example). After 1893 it was national and international events like the Chicago World's Fair that served as more appropriate stages for the promotion and display of new elements of Minnesota's economy.

Selling Minnesota

In 1893, when Lincoln Steffens published "The Shame of the Cities" in *McClure's Magazine*, he exposed political corruption in Minneapolis civic life. But along the avenues of the "White City," as the Chicago World's Fair grounds were called, Minnesota was determined to make a good showing to ensure the state's reputation and prosperity. So organizers decorated the entrance to the Minnesota Building at the World's Fair with a giant painting in grain. In the various industrial and manufacturing buildings, Minnesota displayed premium flour in sacks made of silk and butter daintily sculpted into vines set off by a velvet background concealing a plate of ice. Governor Knute Nelson, the speaker for "Minnesota Day" at the World's Fair, emphasized three main points: the state's healthy climate, its many attractions for immigrants (Nelson was one), and its newest opportunities in agriculture and industry. The latter included iron ore mining in the northern ranges and the rise of mixed farming. In addition to wheat, the state was becoming known for its butter production, with almost 300 creameries in operation. In fact, by the time Chicago's great fair closed, forty butter medals had been awarded to Minnesotans.

This surprising showing represented a major shift from wheat to dairying, already under way in 1885. At that year's New Orleans Industrial and Cotton Centennial, Minnesota's focus was on purebred shorthorn cattle. By the time of the Buffalo Exposition of 1901, Governor Samuel Van Sant was proclaiming that "we have changed our name from the Gopher State to the great Bread and Butter State of the Union." Minnesota featured a replica of Fort Snelling made of homegrown Wealthy apples and a replica of the new State Capitol Building eleven feet long and five feet tall sculpted entirely of Minnesota

The Minnesota State Building at the World's Columbian Exposition in Chicago, 1893.

Minnesotans proudly displayed their agricultural achievements at the St. Louis World's Fair, 1904.

butter. Farmers were learning the benefits of diversification. Repeated harvests of wheat depleted the soil, but a bad wheat year might be a fine one for butter, fruit, sugar beets, potatoes, and other crops. Even at the 1904 St. Louis World's Fair, where Minnesota took a medal for butter sculpture, butter, and flour, organizers also displayed a working model of an iron mine on the Mesabi Range. In the years to come, Minnesota would prosper from both mixed agriculture and a strong mixed economy.

The rivalry between Minneapolis and St. Paul seems here to stay, although on a somewhat lesser scale—if you don't count Governor Jesse Ventura's poke at St. Paul's meandering street plan on late-night TV. Early in his term (1999–2003) Governor Ventura suggested that the city's grid must have been laid down by a drunken Irishman. In doing so, he managed to offend St. Paulites in general and those of Irish immigrant ancestry in particular. But the last serious outbreak of rivalry probably happened in 1893, the year of the Chicago World's Fair. In January, somewhere in the Cascade Mountains of Washington State, the last spike of the Great Northern Railroad track was driven into place. There was no real ceremony: James J. Hill, the railroad's owner, was laid up with rheumatism and stayed home. But St. Paul began to plan "a wild hurrah" to outdo anything Minnesota had seen before: a three-day gala culminating in an evening reception at which anybody—from the governor to the humblest washerwoman—could shake Hill's hand and witness the presentation of an enormous commemorative bowl (it held eighteen quarts) and ladle clearly meant to put Minneapolis's silver tray to shame.

James J. Hill was presented with this silver punch bowl at a St. Paul banquet to honor the completion of his Great Northern line, 1893.

The Fight Goes On

The real centerpiece was a parade through the city during which Hill reviewed five divisions of floats representing the growth of the Northwest, the states and cities linked by the Great Northern Railroad, and a vast array of St. Paul manufacturers and merchants competing for awards of merit. Pulled by matched teams of horses ornamented for the occasion, the floats were masterpieces of art and ingenuity. Powers Dry Goods was represented by a "Barge of Peace" adorned in white, gold, and blue and pulled by all-white horses. An elephant covered in guns and knives towed the float sponsored by hardware wholesaler Farwell, Ozmun, and Kirk. The Hamm Brewing float featured a giant cask and an eagle atop an enormous letter "H." A firm of local furriers had two floats, one showing hunters at work in the Arctic wasteland and the other showing craftsmen making coats from the skins. The parade was worth the $10,000 the city shelled out because *Frank Leslie's Illustrated Newspaper* published pictures of the goings-on to a national audience on June 15, 1893.

But the days of cutthroat competition between Minneapolis and St. Paul were over, along with the effort to boast loudly whenever possible. With progress came a new awareness of a state of great and varied strengths, from "the Zenith City of the Unsalted Seas" (Duluth) to the smallest rural hamlet.

butter sculpture

ON JULY 3, 1880, in honor of the 200th anniversary of Father Louis Hennepin's discovery of the Falls of St. Anthony, Civil War general William Tecumseh Sherman led a procession across the old suspension bridge into downtown Minneapolis, which was dressed up for the Fourth of July celebration in archways made from evergreens.

That commemoration pales in comparison to the gold medal-winning sculpture displayed by Minnesota at the 1904 World's Fair in St. Louis, Missouri: a life-size statue of Father Louis Hennepin, a French voyageur, and a Native American guide preparing to land their canoe at St. Anthony Falls. The detail was exact. A paddle. A bush for tying up their vessel. The tumbling waters of the Mississippi. A feather sticking straight up from the crown of the Indian's head.

Perhaps the statue would have seemed less extraordinary in marble or granite. But it had been carved out of solid Minnesota butter by John K. Daniels, who had created similar masterpieces at the State Fair.

Some art lovers were put off by the sculpture. "Butter is butter," complained one viewer. "Graceful and ethereal as its form may be, one would not hesitate to slice off a nose or a finger to butter his pancakes!" Others simply came to gawk, wondering how long it would take the great explorer and his companions to melt in the blistering St. Louis heat. Minnesotans were heard to brag that, unlike other butter sculptures on exhibit, theirs was the only one made from solid butter. The rest were shams—butter thinly applied over plaster forms. The very idea!

Butter wrappers: the official robes of office for Princess Kay of the Milky Way, first worn at the Minnesota State Fair by Kay the XII in 1966.

IN 1858, DR. WILLIAM Worrall Mayo, a British-born chemist who had studied medicine at the University of Missouri, hung out his shingle in Le Sueur, Minnesota. Like many others, Mayo had come to the state for his health, for the weakness and chills, probably caused by an old case of malaria, that afflicted him every summer. A country doctor, Mayo moved to Rochester, Minnesota, in 1863 when he was named examining surgeon for the State Draft Board. He sent his two sons, Charles and William J., off to medical school to follow in his footsteps.

W. W. Mayo's life changed abruptly on August 21, 1883, when Rochester was devastated by a tornado. Thirty-five people were killed and ninety-seven were injured. Joining forces with the Catholic Sisters of St. Francis, Mayo set up an emergency clinic to care for the casualties. From this modest beginning grew the Mayo Clinic, one of the best-known medical facilities in the world. "The Royal Family"—the three Doctors Mayo—were the Fords and Edisons of modern surgery. They added hotels to their hospital complex for the comfort of patients and their families. They experimented with new surgical and therapeutic techniques. And, in the process, they put Rochester on the map.

In 1915, when the Mayo family tried to give $1.5 million to the University of Minnesota for a joint program, Twin Cities doctors blocked the move for fear their own patients would desert them for southern Minnesota. But it was the prestige of the Mayo Clinic that earned Minnesota a reputation for medical quality and innovation. On that reputation, pacemakers, heart valves, and other devices have become just as important to the diversified modern economy of Minnesota as lumber was in the nineteenth century.

The Doctors Mayo: W. W. and sons Charles and William, ca. 1900.

Jo Lutz Rollins's watercolor of the W. W. Mayo house in Le Sueur.

Postcard view of the new State Capitol building, designed by St. Paul architect Cass Gilbert, ca. 1907.

chapter seven

A THING OF BEAUTY

ON A BRIGHT MAY MORNING in 1896, a distinguished gentleman in a black suit, a necktie, a watch chain, and a vest tore off his jacket, picked up a shovel, and scooped out dirt from the construction site where the new State Capitol was about to rise. The Larpenteurs—Auguste and Mary—took their turns next: they had been the first to homestead this hill in St. Paul. Finally, others in the crowd got into the act, tossing clods of dirt into a waiting wagon. The humble ceremony marked the official arrival of the fine arts in Minnesota.

When the Minnesota Capitol was dedicated in 1905, it was a wonder. Gleaming white, frosted in graceful columns, crowned with a towering dome, and topped off with a gilded chariot and horses, the building was an expression of pride, prosperity—and, perhaps, a little cultural insecurity. The model for St. Paul architect Cass Gilbert's grand design was the Columbian Exposition of 1893, Chicago's "White City." Minnesotans had gone there by the thousands to see a place that looked like ancient Rome, with all the classical trimmings. They saw buildings artistically positioned next to one another and to the landscape in a style that soon evolved into a "City Beautiful" movement across America. In St. Paul, a vast green space led down a hillside toward downtown and the river's old levees. Atop its lofty hill, the capitol stood alone, like

Minnesota Capitol commissioner Channing Seabury breaks ground in 1896 for the new State Capitol. Auguste and Mary Larpenteur, former owners of the property, are the couple immediately behind him.

A study for a mural in the Minnesota State Capitol, 1905. The woman in the center is "Minnesota."

Workmen clean the capitol's *Quadriga* group in 1949.

a beacon of modernity, a model for the duller collection of commercial buildings below.

Inside, the capitol was filled with paintings of graceful ladies and athletic gentlemen draped in togas as symbols of "civilization," "progress," and Minnesota herself. For the most part, the artists were imported from elsewhere. They were fashionable, expensive, and famous, chosen to lend an *aura* (feeling) of culture and splendor to the new capitol. Many of them had painted similar murals on the walls of the Chicago Fair.

The *highfalutin* (fancy) glories of the capitol murals weren't the first real "art" in Minnesota, of course. "Art" was and is a flexible notion.

What Was Minnesota Art?

To the pioneer mothers of Minnesota, the beautiful

stitchery that adorned the quilts that kept their families warm was art too. At local and statewide fairs, paintings were given the same status as quilts, homemade lace, wax flowers, rosemaling, examples of penmanship, curiously patterned stones, and photographs. Art decorated daily life and made it more pleasant. Art was a skill, a knack, a memory of an immigrant's homeland, an image of something familiar or something far away. It was odd, vaguely educational, or just pretty. Art was entertainment. It was the traveling panoramas that set up shop for a day or two and then moved on.

When a huge panoramic canvas was unrolled and slowly pulled across a stage, it looked as though a scene—a moving picture—was passing right before your eyes, as it would if you were taking a stroll. Often, the picture was accompanied by realistic sound effects, music, dramatic shadows, or a commentary by a touring speaker. In the 1870s, panoramas popped up everywhere. John Stevens, a self-taught painter and entrepreneur from Rochester, Minnesota, prowled the state with panorama shows based on the Dakota War of 1862, the Great Chicago Fire of 1871, and other terrors and marvels. Other *itinerant painters* (artists who travel from place to place for work) did portraits, theater curtains, views of towns, primitive advertising materials, and holy images for churches.

Anton Gág, a Bohemian immigrant who settled in New Ulm, Minnesota, in 1879, had all the skills of an itinerant, but managed to make a sparse living in his own community by doing a bit of everything: fancy lettering, altar pieces, and an 1893 panorama showing the heroic defense of his adopted town in the Dakota War. It was in the 1880s and 1890s that increasing numbers of trained artists were attracted to Minnesota. Robert Koehler, another German immigrant, arrived in 1893 to direct the fledgling Minneapolis School of Art. His best-known painting, a view of Hennepin Avenue on a rainy evening, offers a glimpse of a city growing increasingly cosmopolitan with its trolley cars, bicycles, and ordinary people dressed in the latest styles (including Koehler's wife Marie, their son, Edwin, and the family dog). Alexis Fournier, a native of St. Paul, painted telling views of the industrial

Robert Koehler's *Rainy Evening on Hennepin Avenue*, ca. 1910.

edges of the Twin Cities where fashion took the form of the latest in machinery. But, as in the rest of the former frontier, art in gold frames was not a high priority for most Minnesotans. They would pay the modest admission fees to see the plaster casts at the Minneapolis Industrial Exposition, but most of them could not afford to buy original paintings or sculpture and thus support a *cadre* (unified group) of resident artists.

Thomas B. Walker's art gallery on Hennepin Avenue, ca. 1890.

Imported Art

There were at least two bonafide collectors on the Twin Cities scene. In St. Paul, railroad magnate James J. Hill installed an art gallery in his Summit Avenue home in the 1880s. In Minneapolis, lumber baron Thomas B. Walker, who believed that great art had the power to elevate those who saw it, added a gallery to his house in 1880. It was open to the public and enlarged repeatedly. By the 1910s, there were

Artist Alexis Fournier's *St. Paul from Dayton's Bluff,* 1888.

ART MUSEUM, MINNEAPOLIS, MINN.

5A-H1887

The Minneapolis Institute of Arts, ca. 1920, is housed in a building designed by the New York firm of McKim, Meade, and White.

fifteen galleries full of art objects, plus another hundred paintings on exhibit at the public library.

Walker's vast and varied collection, along with Hill's, helped to stimulate a taste for fine art expressed in the lavish decorative plans for the State Capitol. The art on view at the Minneapolis Exposition Building was another impetus to the creation of public spaces for the arts. The Minneapolis Institute of Arts, founded in 1883, moved into a new State Capitol–style building in 1915. Much later, in 1940, T. B. Walker's collection was given a new home at the Walker Art Center.

Minnesota's Writers

While Minnesota commerce and business took off in the post–Civil War years, so did music, literature, theater, and architecture. Some of these arts proved more agreeable to Minnesotans than others. For the state's early writers, their craft had been a matter of chronicling the exciting things they had seen and heard in an unknown land. Seth and Mary Eastman, Henry Rowe Schoolcraft, Harriet Bishop, Frances Densmore, and others described the lives of the Native Americans, as well as the beauty of the region, in a way that inspired a rising generation of

Souvenir postcard of Sinclair Lewis and his boyhood home.

dreamers and immigrants. As Indians gave way to immigrants, O. E. Rolvaag's saga of the hard and lonely Scandinavian settlement of the plains reflected that experience. As massacres and pioneer struggles gave way to peaceful town life, Sinclair Lewis began to *satirize* (mock) the lives and manners of his boyhood neighbors in Sauk Centre, where he was born in 1885. Lewis's *Main Street,* published in 1920, exposed the narrow thinking and cultural isolation of small-town existence, and did so with an ear for the *cadences* (patterns) of midwestern speech and an eye for details of parlor bric-a-brac. Awarded a Pulitzer Prize for his novel, Lewis

went on—in *Babbitt* (1922)—to *parody* (make fun of) Minnesota's boosters, who claimed their midwestern offices and suburban homes were pure slices of paradise.

At the other end of the spectrum was F. Scott Fitzgerald, born in St. Paul in 1896. One of America's greatest novelists, Fitzgerald yearned for the polish and confidence exuded by the wealthy families of Summit Avenue. In early short stories, written before he moved to the East Coast, he painted unforgettable pictures of the State Fair and the Winter Carnival Ice Palace as backgrounds for the doings of debutantes and their beaus. Grace Flandrau, of the same generation as Lewis and Fitzgerald, was highly regarded for her novels of manners that caught the *nuances* (slight differences) of city life in Minnesota's high society. *Being Respectable* (1923), for example, shows women of wealth and leisure gossiping their way through a fancy luncheon alive with perfume, the first strawberries of the season—and a touch of malice. This was the kind of Minnesota that philosopher and economist Thorstein Veblen, a graduate of Carleton College in Northfield, Minnesota, had in mind in his 1899 *Theory of the Leisure Class*. The days of the explorer, of the hardy pioneer, had vanished. In their place was a new, modern Minnesota hemmed in by social ritual and concerns about social status.

Architecture in Minnesota

The pace of building barely kept up with the demand for houses, storefronts, and civic buildings. Many town halls and courthouses across the state were built between 1880 and 1920 in the architectural

St. Paul socialite and author Grace Flandrau, ca. 1920. Flandrau wrote best-selling novels (three of them were made into movies), had her own radio show, and wrote a weekly column for the *St. Paul Dispatch*.

Seventeen-year-old Scott Fitzgerald, second from right, was already a competent playwright when he appeared at the White Bear Yacht Club in a Civil War melodrama he had written titled *The Coward* in 1913.

styles of the day. One of the most distinguished is Minneapolis's City Hall (built 1888–1905), whose tower was the city's first "skyscraper." The enormous building—in the Richardsonian Romanesque style, named for the famous architect of the Pittsburgh Courthouse—commands attention with its spires and turrets and massive round arches, all constructed in a pink granite from Ortonville, Minnesota. Equally *iconic* (symbolic) is St. Paul's City Hall (1931–1932), a major example of the art deco or moderne style. Built in the years between were the neo-Baroque splendors of the Cathedral of St. Paul and the Basilica of St. Mary in Minneapolis, a few baronial stone houses for the urban elite, and the splendid National Farmers Bank in Owatonna (1907–1908) by Louis Sullivan. The Farmers Bank is a jewel box of a building that manages to combine rich surface decoration with structural elements describing just how the bank works as a balance of forces and weights in tension.

The most interesting of Minnesota's architectural achievements of the early twentieth century, however,

City Hall was once Minneapolis's tallest building.

The Cathedral of St. Paul by architect Emmanuel Masqueray.

are far more *utilitarian* (practical). You'll find a residential example on Milwaukee Avenue in Minneapolis, a streetscape of one-and-a-half-story brick homes built between 1885 and 1904. This is a working man's neighborhood, showing how elegance can be achieved at modest cost.

A second, commercial example is almost invisible. In 1887, architect Leroy Buffington of Minneapolis applied for a patent on a twenty-eight-story metal frame for tall buildings. Buffington's idea was to hang walls of glass or masonry from a skeleton like so many curtains—the same method used in constructing tall buildings today. Many of the older buildings on the University of Minnesota campus—Pillsbury Hall, Burton Hall—as well as houses for the wealthy emerged from Buffington's drawing board in all kinds of period styles. But he continued to defend his patent for the modern skyscraper, without much success. Finally, in 1929, upon payment of a voluntary *royalty* (payment) to Buffington, the Rand (later Dain) Tower in downtown Minneapolis was

The art deco–style St. Paul City and County Building, 1937.

A working man's house on Milwaukee Avenue, Minneapolis, ca. 1910.

constructed by Chicago architects according to his innovative structural design.

The last noteworthy piece of made-in-Minnesota architecture of the era is strictly utilitarian: the Peavey-Haglin concrete grain elevator on Highway 100 in St. Louis Park. The reinforced concrete grain elevator was designed by Frank Peavey to replace the older method of storing grain in wooden or stone silos, which were subject to fire and explosion. The concrete elevator

The Rand (Dain) Tower in Minneapolis was built according to the skyscraper patent held by architect Leroy Buffington.

The cylindrical Peavey-Haglin concrete elevator in St. Louis Park, ca. 1900, revolutionized grain storage.

proved strong enough to resist most disasters. Soon, other circular towers sprouted across America, wherever grain or coal needed to be stored and transferred.

The Performing Arts

In music and theater, Minnesotans were an eager audience for performers on tour. All but the smallest towns had their music halls or opera houses, visited by actors and musicians who were the celebrities of their day. Pictures of Ole Bull, Adelina Patti, Joseph Jefferson, and Dan Emmett advertised products and filled scrapbooks of adoring fans beginning in the 1860s. Edwin Booth, the most famous actor of his era, appeared in Shakespeare's plays. And *Uncle Tom's Cabin,* the theatrical sensation of its day, made audiences scream with terror and delight when Little Eva crossed the ice-choked river on stage, pursued by real bloodhounds. Via new railroad lines, touring minstrel and variety shows brought entertainment to Stillwater, Red Wing, Winona, Duluth, Moorhead, St. Cloud, Wadena, and forty-odd other towns that had theater buildings in the 1880s.

Theatergoers who supported *temperance* (little or no drinking of alcohol) occasionally objected to a familiar drama based on the story of Rip van Winkle because the hero wanted a drink when he awakened from his lengthy snooze. In the Twin Cities, the theater season opened in the early fall because it was then that visitors to the State Fair crowded the streets after hours. A play called *In Old Kentucky* was dusted off every autumn for eighteen consecutive years especially for the farm families visiting from out-of-town. When movies began to displace live actors after 1910, theaters were reborn as motion picture houses.

Opera house, Brainerd, ca. 1905.

St. Paul's Grand Opera House on Third Street (now Kellogg Boulevard), ca. 1870.

Players take the stage of the Metropolitan Opera House, Duluth, ca. 1910.

Art and Minnesota's Past

Cities had their charms, but the flavor of Minnesota's small towns around 1900 was beautifully re-created in the children's novels of Maud Hart Lovelace, born in 1892. Her *Betsy-Tacy* books were a favorite of little girls from the time the series started in 1940. They were based on the sights and pleasures of life in Lovelace's hometown of Mankato (renamed "Deep Valley"): the Carnegie Library, Lincoln Park, picnics, musicales, amateur plays, and, above all, nature. Her young heroines, she wrote, "had the whole hill for a playground. And not just that green slope. There were hills all around them."

Wanda Gág of New Ulm (born in 1893), the daughter of artist Anton Gág and a gifted painter in her own right, took the old Bohemian fairy tales she had heard at home and translated them into illustrated books for children. Although the characters in *Millions of Cats* (1928) and her other popular books look like they come from the Old World, the hilly landscapes are those of New Ulm, polished into images of a Minnesota heaven on earth.

There are two excellent means of imagining Minnesota as it was in the exciting decades at the turn of the nineteenth century. Picture postcards, which came into general use after the first mass-produced color cards were sold at the Chicago World's Fair of 1893, amounted to a national craze. People mailed them home—for 2 cents—from vacations, of course. But many simply collected them, like baseball cards, to remind them of wonders they had seen or hoped to see. By today's standards, some pictures on the postcards seem strange: the streets of tiny hamlets, the interiors of new stores, Anoka's annual Potato Palace, butter sculpture, even an ad for a Dodge Center real estate agent picturing a statue of "Miss Minne Sota,"

put together from sheaves of grain. Other images included civic statues, tall buildings, the State Fair, and the State Capitol. In other words, the postcards show the great and small, or whatever Minnesotans found important, newsworthy, or fascinating at the time.

The second window on Minnesota in the era of James J. Hill comes in the mystery novels of architectural historian Larry Millett. By bringing British author Arthur Conan Doyle's Sherlock Holmes, England's greatest fictional detective, to Minnesota as an ally of

In *Millions of Cats* a very old man goes off in search of a kitten to keep him and his wife company and returns with "hundreds of cats, thousands of cats, millions and billions and trillions of cats."

Postcards were a great fad of the early 1900s. This one shows downtown Anoka's famous corn and potato "palace."

the imperious "Empire Builder," Millett introduces the reader to several major "mysteries" of that time. Together, Holmes and his local pals solve the case of a stolen Minnesota runestone and a murder at the St. Paul Ice Palace. They find the cause of a massive fire in the timber country around Hinckley, and they track down the killer of a union member in the midst of a plot to blow up a Minneapolis flour mill. Using his knowledge of the buildings' layouts and the historical characters and issues of the 1890s and 1900s, Millett helps the reader see the magic and mystery in the streets Minnesotans pass through every day. That's one of the things art does best: it stimulates the imagination, the memory, and the feelings. It makes us more fully human.

Art can also be fun. Popular or mass-produced art, like the postcard, also came into its own around 1900. Suddenly, everybody could own art in the form of dimestore sheet music, mail-order pianos and phonographs, and pictures in magazines. The newspapers added comic cartoons. And finally, the radio presented programming that ran the *gamut* (range) from grand opera to the serial adventures of lovelorn secretaries. For better or for worse, the twentieth century had dawned in Minnesota.

This early advertising postcard from Dodge Center shows "Miss Minne Sota" made of grain, 1907.

Christmas Eve in the Bohemian Flats by S. Chatwood Burton, 1919.

ONE OF THE PROBLEMS that faced many American artists in the early 1900s was that their country seemed so ordinary, so unpicturesque. The same scenery that had enchanted Europeans a century before looked boring to ambitious young painters brought up in Minnesota.

But one spot along the Mississippi River opposite the University of Minnesota qualified as exotic and worth painting. It was known as the Bohemian Flats, although the little shacks were populated by Finns, Danes, Slovaks, Poles, Austrians, Czechs, and a flock of Irish called the Connemaras, who arrived as a group in the 1880s. The Flats was a working-class neighborhood, lacking running water, sewer lines, and electricity but rich in ethnic tradition.

Every morning, residents trudged up the seventy-nine wooden steps that led to the Washington Avenue trolley and to jobs as bartenders, shopgirls, janitors, and embroiderers. But every night they came home to little vegetable gardens, a few goats, folk music and Old World holiday festivities—and tiny houses that made up for what they lacked in comforts by the bright colors lavished on doors and window frames. Until the area was torn down for a municipal barge terminal in the early 1930s, it truly was Minnesota's Bohemia.

Artist Dewey Albinson called it "the one bit of atmosphere in the whole city of Minneapolis." Professor S. Chatwood Burton, who taught art at the University of Minnesota, rented a cottage there for use as a studio. Everybody recognized his hideaway because Burton painted the door a brilliant sky blue.

Minnesota artists also painted one another. Dewey Albinson painted this portrait of painter Frances Cranmer Greenman about 1925.

Dewey Albinson sketches a boatman on Lake Superior, 1922.

penumbra theatre

ONE OF THE MOST INFLUENTIAL Minnesota theater companies is Penumbra, a product of the black arts movement and the Black Power movement of the 1960s. Founder and artistic director Lou Bellamy speaks of the "new sense of self, a new cultural awareness" among African Americans arising from that era. That "new cultural awareness" was the inspiration behind Penumbra. Centered in the Selby/Dale neighborhood and the old Rondo district in St. Paul, Penumbra is one of only three professional African American theaters

The Penumbra quilt mural reflects the history of the theater, the historic Rondo neighborhood, and the African American experience. For an explanation of each quilt square, check out www.penumbratheatre.org.

Artistic Director Lou Bellamy founded the Penumbra Theatre in 1976.

in the nation. It is dedicated to depicting human experience from the perspective of black artists such as Pulitzer Prize winner August Wilson, who lived in St. Paul for twelve years and staged his first professional production at Penumbra.

In 2008, Penumbra will collaborate with the Guthrie Theater of Minneapolis on Wilson's *Gem of the Ocean,* one of the dramas in the late playwright's epic ten-play cycle. Although Wilson's work has appeared on Broadway and London stages, only one of his plays has been previously performed at the Guthrie. This partnership marks a fresh affirmation of the relevance of all of Minnesota's communities to the life and vitality of the state.

The fountain-sculpture *Spoonbridge and Cherry* by pop artist Claes Oldenburg and Coosje Van Bruggen, his wife and collaborator, anchors the Minneapolis Sculpture Garden. Fabricated at two shipbuilding yards in New England, the spoon weighs 5,800 pounds and the cherry, 1,200. The century-old Basilica of Saint Mary is framed in the background.

chapter eight

MODERN MINNESOTA

IN 1893, WHEN MINNESOTANS trooped off in force to see the wonders of the World's Fair at Chicago, a select few attended the lecture given there by Professor Frederick Jackson Turner to a group of historians. The so-called "Turner thesis" argued that America's democratic institutions had been shaped by the existence of the frontier. Out on the edges of civilization, people were forced to improvise their own rough justice. And if things got too civilized—as the cowboy movie would later insist, over and over again—they could pick up and move on into the next town, the next valley, the next sunset.

When Turner spoke, the frontier had officially closed. There was no more free land for the claiming. Although it would be almost a hundred years before American critics began to complain that every place was now just like every other, parts of the United States had already begun to seem more alike with the rapid spread of technologies, trading opportunities, and great national responsibilities. In the twentieth century, Minnesota was no longer defined by French voyageurs, Indian wars, railroad magnates, flour mills, Civil War regiments, and bonanza farms. Things had begun to change at a dizzying speed.

Good News, Bad News

An example of Minnesota in the news: In May 1927, the lanky young son of a Minnesota Congressman flew alone across the Atlantic to Paris. Charles A. Lindbergh, Jr.—"Lucky Lindy"—was the biggest news story of the half-century. He was modest, handsome, brave, and shy, and came from a place out there on the prairies called Little Falls, Minnesota. And he carried with him the good wishes of a nation and the

Charles A. Lindbergh, Jr. poses with his *Spirit of St. Louis,* ca. 1927.

Northwest Airlines became one of Minnesota's largest companies. This passenger plane was used in the 1950s.

banner of a new era of winged flight, speed, power, and boundaries that no longer mattered much. The trails and streams that once brought immigrants to Minnesota inch by inch were little more than a blur beneath the wings of Lindbergh's silvery *Spirit of St. Louis.* Time sped up as distance disappeared. By the 1960s and 1970s, Minnesota found itself a leader in a high-tech revolution and the Orient was only hours away on a Northwest Airlines jet.

Bad news: On October 19, 1902, the body of Jim Younger was found by police officers in a dingy room at the Hotel Reardon in downtown St. Paul. Finally paroled from Stillwater Prison, he had shot himself in the head with a pistol during a bout of depression. His brother Cole thought that Jim had never recovered from wounds suffered during their capture near Madelia, Minnesota, in the aftermath of the Northfield

bank robbery of 1876. By 1902, the shoot-'em-up era of the Wild West bad man had come and gone—at least until Prohibition and the Great Depression created a new class of urban gangsters and whiskey smugglers who hid out in St. Paul.

Isolationism and Fear

On April 22, 1917, the governor signed into law a bill establishing a Commission of Public Safety to ensure the loyalty of Minnesotans on the home front during World War I. The commission banned German books, registered aliens and the foreign-born, searched out anyone whose patriotism seemed questionable, harassed *pacifists* (antiwar activists), spied on Socialists and union members, and suppressed strikes. Part of a larger national phenomenon called the "Red Scare," Minnesota's hysteria over alien influence lasted into the 1920s and 1930s. It wore a variety of guises, including Ku Klux Klan activity against "radicals," Catholics, and foreigners, and a bitter split between workers and the new corporate face of business culminating in the violent Minneapolis truckers' strike of 1934. Change came only at a price.

Despite, or because of, Minnesota's participation in World Wars I and II and the Korean War, isolationism came into conflict with America's growing global role. Despite the immigrant roots of Minnesota, that same suspicion of outsiders has led to prejudice and fear of difference. Jews, the Hmong, Somali and Russian refugees, Arabs, African Americans, and Latinos all have felt the sting of being newcomers, aliens in a white, well-off, English-speaking and increasingly conservative community. Visitors often remark on the friendliness and warmth of their welcome—a phenomenon known as "Minnesota Nice." Those who have come to stay sometimes find that beneath the "Nice" lurks a core of solid ice. With every change comes a new reassertion of stability.

Modern Industry

Stability is good for business, and modern business thrived in Minnesota during and after World War II. Minnesota Mining and Manufacturing—better known as 3M—marketed Scotch-brand tape in the early 1930s and developed industrial and military applications for its products in wartime. The company promoted a growing line of consumer products afterward, including the ever-popular Post-it Note. Honeywell, Control Data, and IBM gave the world its first

St. Paul's 3M (Minnesota Mining and Manufacturing Company) used the occasion of Minnesota's participation in the 1991 World Series to promote its Post-it Notes in the IDS (Investors Diversified Services) Crystal Court in downtown Minneapolis.

Betty Crocker spoon logo.

computers. Medtronic and its rivals invented heart pacemakers and other medical devices. General Mills introduced Betty Crocker, who became known as America's First Lady of Food. More than a generation later, Pillsbury launched the giggling Doughboy. IDS reinvented investing for the average American. Dayton's morphed into Target, America's hippest retailer. Cargill became the largest privately owned grain distributor in the world. All of it, from army K-rations to stem cells and organ transplants, has been enhanced by research conducted at the University of Minnesota, research that transcends state and national boundaries.

Minnesota business operates in a global marketplace. So does agriculture. In 1970, Professor Norman Borlaug of the University of Minnesota, father of the "Green Revolution," won the Nobel Prize for his work on new strains of hybrid wheat, with much larger yields. Although a great deal has been lost in the transition from the family farm to corporate megafarms, something has been gained too: Minnesota's growing ability to feed a hungry Third World and to use crops as the basis for new products, including plastics and fuels. Soybeans and millet grow in former wheat fields. Turkeys have replaced wheat as the cash crop over much of southern Minnesota. The potatoes and the starch industry of the Anoka Sand Plain have all but vanished. But the relationship between pigs and corn propels the butchering and packing operations at Austin, Minnesota, where Hormel invented Spam, the canned meat that made the company world famous in the 1940s, both on the frontlines and the homefront. Over time, populations have shifted from the small towns of farm country to the Twin Cities and its growing suburbs. But the seesaw balance between agriculture and industry that has served Minnesota so well during past times of economic stress continues to provide stability, continuity, and a strong sense of rootedness.

"The Good Life in Minnesota"

On August 13, 1973, a new issue of *Time* magazine hit the newsstands. Read by an estimated 4.25 million Americans each week, *Time* both confirmed and initiated trends. That week, the cover story

Norman Borlaug of the University of Minnesota headed the "Green Revolution." He was awarded the 1970 Nobel Prize for building peace through increasing the world's food supply.

Turkeys have become a major cash crop in Minnesota.

was Minnesota—specifically, "The Good Life in Minnesota," and the cover boy was Governor Wendell Anderson, smiling broadly, wearing a lumberjack-plaid shirt, and holding up a trophy-sized Northern pike just plucked from the lake behind him. And just what was the "good life" in the state? It was the essence of Minnesota, a place of beauty, harmony, public-minded millionaires, a sound economy, and plenty of big fish. Indeed, by the early 1970s, tourism was one of state's most important industries. From an association of ma-and-pa cabin resorts established in the 1910s to the multimillion-dollar industry at the heart of the *Time* story, Minnesota tourism made use of the land up north that had not yet been clear-cut or mined to attract Americans eager to enjoy the cool quiet of a lake, a stand of trees, and a northern sky.

Although tourists from the South had come to St. Anthony Falls in the summers before the Civil War, more

Governor Wendell Anderson (third from right) wears a historic voyageur costume at Fort Snelling, 1974.

BURLEY'S FURNISHED LOG CABINS. ELY. MINN.   42570

A postcard view of Burley's Cabins in Ely, ca. 1940.

recent visitors are part of a growing awareness of what was lost in the rush to capture the natural wealth of Minnesota. The Boundary Waters Canoe Area in northeast Minnesota, created by the 1964 Wilderness Act, opened more than a million acres of forest and lakes to visitors and helped promote ecological activism. (Laws imposed in 1978 that banned cars, motorboats, and other vehicles from the BWCA remain controversial in some quarters.) This was territory once visited by voyageurs. Now it welcomed modern tourists longing for a taste of life long ago—the good life of the nation's dreams. Ely, a former mining town and now the gateway to the BWCA, asserted its new identity in the person of Will Steger, the colorful polar adventurer who makes his home there.

But there was more to Minnesota than fishing and camping, as *Time* was quick to note. Thanks in part to local *philanthropists* (charitable donors) and corporations, Minnesota was a public-spirited place alive with art and culture. Along the gently curved Nicollet Mall in downtown Minneapolis (designed by Lawrence Halprin in 1958–1962), the best in modern architecture was set off by trees and sculpture. The skyline of the business district had once been dominated by the spires of City Hall and the Foshay Tower, a thirty-two-story copy of the Washington Monument that was unveiled in 1929. In 1973, both buildings would be overshadowed by the IDS Tower, Philip Johnson's architectural masterpiece, a Minnesota icon that is, quite possibly, as one commentator has written, "the most beautiful tall building in the United States." St. Paul pursued a different course, with a campaign to restore and preserve its turn-of-the-century courthouse, reopened in the

Built in 1931 at a cost of $3.7 million, the thirty-two-story Foshay Tower in Minneapolis was Minnesota's first true skyscraper.

The IDS Building, reflecting the Northwest Center, in Minneapolis.

1970s as the Landmark Center. Located at the head of Rice Park, the building is the centerpiece of a collection of old and new buildings (and their skyways) that together form a graceful version of modern urbanism. And, *Time* marveled, wherever there was a skyscraper or a sliver of parkland, there was bound to be a lake.

Suburbia and Shopping

In the postwar years, the mushroom growth of leafy suburbs demanded as much attention as the core cities themselves. The brothers Dayton, of Dayton's Department Store, hired architect Victor Gruen to give the Minneapolis suburb of Edina the conveniences of the old downtowns in a different setting. The result was Southdale, the nation's first enclosed shopping mall. It defied Minnesota's abrupt change of seasons, of course, but the planners also wanted to make Southdale an urban center for a newly dispersed population. In addition to shops, the mall had sidewalk cafes, a post office, distractions for children—and the added luxury of artworks by some of the nation's finest designers. It was an indoor model for what the Nicollet Mall would later become, and like the Minneapolis mall, Southdale stimulated development in Edina, where apartment complexes, health centers, theaters, and libraries soon took shape.

The late-century counterpart to Southdale is the massive Mall of America in Bloomington, which opened to enormous publicity in 1992. It remains the largest enclosed mall in the country, with more than 500 stores, an indoor amusement park, and a fortress wall of surrounding parking ramps. As architecture,

At 2.5 million square feet, the Mall of America is the world's largest indoor mall. Opened in 1992, it attracts 40 million visitors annually.

Fans tear down the scoreboard after the Vikings were defeated in the last football game played at Met Stadium, 1981. The Mall of America now occupies the site.

the Mall of America is undistinguished: the building looks inward, where the real attractions await. These include a series of rotundas that hold vast numbers of people, making the mall a gathering place for community and charitable events. But by virtue of its size and proximity to the Minneapolis–St. Paul International Airport, the Mall of America is also proof that Minnesota is not "fly-over country," best seen from 30,000 feet up.

We're All Above Average

In Minnesota's early history, boosters found it necessary to defend their state from reports of terrible climate, poor growing conditions, and dangers lurking behind every tree. Now, with the help of *Time,* Southdale, and Tyrone Guthrie's original theater (designed by the visionary local architect Ralph Rapson), Minnesota in the 1970s could begin to boast in earnest about its sophisticated cultural scene, its close relationship to nature, and its industrious, intelligent inhabitants (represented by the grinning Governor Anderson). But it was not considered appropriately "Minnesota" to boast too loudly. Instead, during the late twentieth century a kind of *self-deprecating*

Garrison Keillor (right) and cast members on the set of his national *Prairie Home Companion* radio show.

humor (poking fun at one's self) came to define what it meant to be a Minnesotan. The chief representative of this trend was Garrison Keillor, of Anoka and the University of Minnesota, whose *Prairie Home Companion*—a revival of old-time variety shows with an *irreverent* (humorously disrespectful) modern twist—began to air on public radio in 1974. Minnesota's children, said Keillor with his usual false modesty, were "all above average." And so too were the other personalities who began to represent Minnesota to a media-driven America, like TV's MacGyver (played by Richard Dean Anderson of Minneapolis), who could find his way out of any jam with a paper clip and a stick of gum. Then there was Mary Tyler

The original Guthrie Theater, designed by Ralph Rapson, opened in Minneapolis in 1963.

Moore, that intrepid producer for a fictional Minneapolis TV station. She flung her winter hat to the heavens in a gesture of weather-defying exuberance—and then, as one of TV's first feminist heroines, worked through her problems with unfailing, smiling pluck.

Politics, Prince, and the World Series

In the 1960s and 1970s Hubert Humphrey and Walter Mondale served as vice presidents under Lyndon Johnson and Jimmy Carter, respectively. Humphrey and Mondale were men of political courage who were passionate about civil rights. They had good sense, good will, and boundless humor more obvious in defeat than in victory: they were true Minnesotans. But there was surprising variety in the emerging definition of a Minnesotan. Prince Nelson Rogers was a true Minnesotan too, in all the purple splendor of his revolutionary rock music: a black kid from Minneapolis with the manners of a Norwegian matron, a creative force that brought young pilgrims by the thousands to his purple house in Chanhassen. Then there was the feisty, pregnant sheriff with the "you-bet-cha" accent in the Coen brothers' 1996 hit movie, *Fargo.* And *North Country* (1984), *Grumpy Old Men* (1993), and a score of hockey movies that captured the natural scenery of Minnesota along with something of the social scenery of quiet put-downs, hard work, and something a little *different* about the characters, besides their accents.

Harry Blackmun and Warren Burger were different, the other "Minnesota twins" who served simultaneously on the U.S. Supreme Court during the scandalous Nixon era. Eugene McCarthy was different, a

The Mary Tyler Moore statue in downtown Minneapolis recalls her enormously popular 1970s TV sitcom, *The Mary Tyler Moore Show.*

Two Minnesotans served as U.S. vice presidents: Walter Mondale (left) for Jimmy Carter and Hubert Humphrey for Lyndon Johnson.

Minnesota senator Eugene McCarthy was a protest leader during the Vietnam War. Here, McCarthy poses with his father in 1958.

senator, poet, and pacifist who led a crusade against the Vietnam War. Gerry Spiess of White Bear Lake was different, an explorer who set out to sail alone across the Atlantic Ocean in *Yankee Girl*, his ten-foot-long homemade boat in 1979. The Minnesota Vikings were different, with their horns and ferocity and nary a Super Bowl victory. So was Jessica Lange, homegrown movie star from Cloquet, who lived quietly in Minnesota along the St. Croix River between forays into Hollywood and New York. So was Patty Wetterling, mother of eleven-year-old Jacob, abducted from St. Joseph in 1989, who turned her grief into a foundation to save other vanished children. The Minnesota Twins of the American League, a small-market team with small hopes, unaccountably won the World Series in 1987 and again in 1991. Miracles happen. Just ask the mostly Minnesota kids coached by St. Paul native Herb Brooks, who accomplished a "Miracle on Ice" at the 1980 Olympics by winning the gold medal against all odds—and the formidable USSR team.

Minnesota had its share of disasters along the way, from the bitter labor problems of the 1930s to the 1985 packing-plant strike in Austin that left the city divided and exhausted. All the fabled bad weather in Minnesota history was summed up by the Halloween blizzard of 1991. Most of those who lived through it, however, remembered the kindness of neighbors and strangers who shoveled and dug and pulled. Duluth still debates the reasons why the ore carrier *Edmund Fitzgerald* sank in a November storm on Lake Superior in 1975, taking twenty-nine crew members to the bottom. And will Minnesota ever know who kidnapped Virginia Piper of Orono in 1972, chained

This Minnesota Vikings professional football team was the first to play in the Super Bowl, in 1969. During the 1970s head coach Bud Grant steered the "Purple People Eaters" to four Super Bowls with star athletes that included linemen Carl Eller, Jim Marshall, and Alan Page.

her to a tree, and disappeared into thin air with a $1 million ransom? Or who smothered heiress Elizabeth Congdon (and her nurse) in her Duluth mansion, leaving behind a case so fraught with uncertainties that the true villains may never be known?

But mainly, Minnesota in the twentieth century was a textbook illustration of "the good life." The State Fair still chugged along, drawing ever bigger crowds every August with the promise of pigs, beauty queens, deep-fried anything-on-a-stick, midway rides, amazing products, and hopeful politicians. The fair has been a defining part of Minnesota since before statehood. In recent years, it has taken on the task of showing city folk where food comes from. The beautiful State Capitol still dominates its hill in St. Paul. It's the place where Minnesotans rally when they're angry or happy or sorrowful. The Winter Carnival and the Aquatennial spawn enough parades and goofiness for their respective seasons. On the Fourth of July, make-believe soldiers dressed in the uniforms of Josiah Snelling's day fire off their cannon in the old fort. When Fort Snelling was built, July 4 was the nation's only holiday. Today, Independence Day is observed by Ojibwe and Dakota bands, by African Americans, by Somalis, by Hmong and Vietnamese, by Mexicans, and all the rest: the citizens of Minnesota, of "L'étoile du Nord"—a real northern star.

frank b. kellogg

Frank B. Kellogg, oil painting by C. B. Pereira, ca. 1930.

THE POLITICAL HISTORY of Minnesota is peppered with men and women of feisty independence and generosity of spirit. Whatever their party affiliations, they have brought humanity, common sense, and passion for the public good to their work as leaders on the state and national level. One such figure is Frank B. Kellogg, a one-time handyman and self-educated lawyer from Rochester, Minnesota, who went on to make his fortune in St. Paul representing the railroading,

iron, and steel interests that were developing the Mesabi Range. Despite his pro-business sentiments, however, Kellogg won national fame by serving as Theodore Roosevelt's prosecutor in antitrust actions against the Union Pacific Railroad and Standard Oil. In other words, Kellogg was not afraid to take on the regulation of the very industries he had once served.

Elected to the Senate as a Republican in 1917, Kellogg was a staunch supporter of Democrat Woodrow Wilson's campaign to establish a League of Nations in the interests of world peace. Under Calvin Coolidge, Kellogg became secretary of state in 1925. In that diplomatic role, he was one of the authors of the Kellogg-Briand Pact of 1928—sixty-four countries signed the pledge—renouncing war as an instrument of national policy. For his tireless work on behalf of mankind, Kellogg was honored with the 1929 Nobel Peace Prize.

"the good neighbor"

MANY HISTORIANS BELIEVE that the power of the media has been a major force in making the United States into a more *homogeneous* (look-alike) place. In other words, magazines, radio, movies, and television with a national reach have meant that everybody gets the same dose of news, ads, attitudes, and celebrity antics. But if the mass media can wipe out regional differences, they can also reinforce them. That is certainly the case with WCCO Radio. The station has served Minnesota for more than eighty years, thanks to its "clear channel" frequency of 830 kHz on the dial, which allows its signal to reach into every corner of the state (and a huge chunk of North America besides).

Founded in 1922, the station had a rocky start. It closed briefly in 1924 and was acquired by Washburn-Crosby Company, a milling firm that later became General Mills. Washburn-Crosby changed the call letters to WCCO and "The Good Neighbor" was in business, offering a daily menu of farm reports, weather warnings (signaled by an unforgettable "klaxon" sound), school closing announcements, wacky comedy, live banter at the Minnesota State Fair, cooking tips and, more recently, traffic reports for frustrated commuters.

On the most basic level, 'CCO's programming recited a long list of place names every day. Charlie Boone and Roger Erickson taught us how to pronounce "Edina" and where, exactly, Tower was, and how cold it got that day in International Falls ("Icebox of the Nation"). A joke told on air at 7 a.m. would be repeated in offices and cafes all over the state by 8 a.m. WCCO was the friendly voice that united Minnesotans. In times of joy and trouble, it made us one.

Top right: WCCO regular Clelland Card broadcasting his early morning program "Almanac," ca. 1940.

Right: Hubert H. Humphrey reading comics on the radio, 1946. Humphrey, who would later become vice president of the United States under Lyndon Johnson (1965–1969), was mayor of Minneapolis at the time.

A large regional museum built into the Mississippi River's limestone bluffs facing downtown St. Paul, the Science Museum of Minnesota invites learners of all ages to experience their changing world through science.

chapter nine

WHAT'S NEXT FOR MINNESOTA?

ONE HUNDRED AND FIFTY YEARS from now—in 2158—Minnesota will probably assemble an official committee to observe its *tercentenary* (three hundredth birthday). Citizens may even look back at the way the state celebrated its sesquicentennial in 2008. Thus far, Minnesotans have never been reluctant to wear pioneer costumes, visit historic sites, take another look at local relics, and pause to reflect on the lives and deeds of its founding mothers and fathers. Sometimes, we look back to measure just how far we've come. In the recent past, the notion that there is something to be learned from history has become unfashionable. At the same time nostalgia for the good old days and a hankering for antiques plucked from ancestral homesteads have never been stronger. But if history becomes only a pleasant escape from the present—if it becomes *irrelevant* (unrelated) to understanding ourselves—how will we ever summon the wisdom and courage to change for the better? History is about looking back. Yet it is also about looking forward and eagerly steering an educated course into tomorrow.

History teaches us that Minnesota politics has always been volatile, a struggle between competing groups, from fur traders and railroad builders to civil rights leaders and social activists. More recently, the political scene has witnessed the same rapid cycles of change, but that change is sometimes marked by a lack of respect that has driven many citizens away from the process. Although Minnesota still has one of the highest voter turnout rates in the nation, the passion for public service has waned. Where are the new Hubert Humphreys, the Harry Blackmuns and the Warren Burgers, the Henry Sibleys and the William LeDucs?

In a sense, the state has always been two Minnesotas: one urban, one rural. The farmer's interests were not always those of the merchant or the factory worker. Today, cities find themselves in competition with their own suburbs for the money to fund safer streets and better schools. Who should share the social obligation to care for those in need? Beginning in the 1950s, the flight to the suburbs for "the good life" has had the effect of stranding the poor, the elderly, and minorities in inner cities that struggle to find the resources required to alleviate their problems. As a state, Minnesota has not yet addressed the inequalities of income that threaten to create a permanent inner-city underclass. Racial minorities, including African Americans, Native Americans, Latinos, and Asians are disproportionately trapped in a poverty that threatens to divide the cities into exclusive neighborhoods of multimillion-dollar houses and condominiums within sight of misery and urban decay.

The current energy crisis will not disappear overnight, either, without action on the part of Minnesota's determined citizens. The state has been slow to support public transportation that could reduce both oil dependency and pollution. Already, the experts say, global warming hastened by the use of fossil fuels has changed the climate of the Midwest. How will Minnesota agriculture fare when the winters are short and warm and the summers are long and hot? Biofuels grown and produced in Minnesota seem to be part of the answer to America's dependence on oil. Wind farms are also possible sources of energy across the plains. But all of these issues require a long-term perspective on history. Minnesota needs to remember its trolleys and trains and steamboats. It needs to remember forests, soil, and landscapes destroyed in the haste to exploit natural resources for short-term gain.

Minnesota has always been a part of a global marketplace. Its furs were sold in London and Paris; its flour was traded for premium prices in Warsaw and Minsk. Its lumber built the homes of the American West. Its medical and computer technology has reached every part of the world. Minnesota products from Cheerios and pacemakers to Spam and Scotch tape are sold everywhere. The Mall of America is an international tourist destination. Minnesota authors and artists receive universal accolades. But globalization has brought problems of its own, including a decline in traditional *blue collar* (labor) jobs. At the same time, the lower-paying service and office economies have boomed. More families depend on two paychecks to survive. It has become harder to get ahead in a familiar place that suddenly seems so unfamiliar.

In the past decade or so, places devoted to culture and the arts have flourished, in terms of their architectural settings. The Minnesota Historical Society, the Science Museum of Minnesota, the Weisman Art Museum, the Walker Art Center, the Guthrie Theater, the Minneapolis Public Library, and the Minneapolis Institute of Arts all have splendid new buildings designed by the superstars of architecture, including Cesar Pelli, Frank Gehry, and Michael Graves. Other institutions, including the Saint Paul Public Library, have undergone major renovation. For a state in which the arts arrived late and without a great deal of initial distinction, Minnesota's rise to a position of leadership in the arts has been astonishing. Visitors to the state—those who get no farther than a downtown hotel—often remark on two striking features of the Twin Cities: art and the greenery, the latter concentrated in one of the most extensive and well-planned park systems in the world. Visitors to Minnesota who come with fishing rods and snowshoes are apt to be looking for nature, as Henry Sibley and Alexander Ramsey and Henry Schoolcraft saw it, at the very beginning, in the Boundary Waters Canoe Area, in its unspoiled splendor. Minnesota is past and present in happy alignment.

But Minnesota—the idea of Minnesota—is as fragile as a wisp of smoke from a Native American campfire. What Minnesotans are, what Minnesotans aspire to be, must be nurtured, treasured, and they must be committed to the change that has always defined the state's collective culture. In 2006, the legislature named the Honey Crisp apple the official Minnesota State Apple. There was a time when nobody believed it was possible to grow an apple in so cold and inhospitable a place. Minnesotans learned. Minnesotans need to keep on learning.

Comprising more than one million acres, Minnesota's Boundary Waters Canoe Area was carved by great glaciers that left behind rugged cliffs and canyons, gentle hills and towering rock formations, rocky shores and sandy beaches. Its several thousand lakes and streams contain more than twelve hundred miles of canoe routes, allowing visitors to canoe, portage, and camp in the spirit of the French voyageurs.

a cultural mosaic

ONE OF THE MOST VISIBLE signs of change in Minnesota over the past twenty-five years has been demographic—the arrival of immigrants and refugees from all parts of the world. State Senator Mee Moua, whose family came from the mountains of Laos in the aftermath of the Vietnam War, says that "to be an AmerICAN is to know that I CAN." In Minnesota, she and the thousands of Hmong people resettled by war have seized the opportunity to find a new identity as Asian Americans, Americans, and Minnesotans. The state has become a stage upon which the eternal drama of *displacement* (a forced move) and self-determination is played out once again.

Some groups, like the Somalis, are newcomers. Others have lived in Minnesota for many years, sometimes unnoticed by the EuroAmerican majority. Native Americans and African Americans, for example, have been here from the start, by choice or forced migration. Latinos have been here since the mid-nineteenth century, their numbers swollen in recent years by political upheaval south of the U.S. border and the chance for a better life in the northland. Overseas adoptions have also contributed to a greater diversity in our school population.

With immigration comes complex problems too. Are newcomers "taking jobs" away from "true" Minnesotans—or are they filling positions that no one else will take? Are they draining state service budgets—or are they contributing to the tax base that improves services for everyone?

Without doubt, newcomers have brought a cultural *renaissance* (rebirth) to many parts of the state with their arts, customs, costumes, and food. Minnesota lives in a global economy now, and so the state has become an outpost of the global village in the center of the continent, rich in hope and promise.

protecting natural resources

THE HEALTH OF THE PLANET is one of the principal concerns of this generation. We must learn to protect our natural resources—resources in which Minnesota abounds.

During its annual May Day Parade in 2007, In the Heart of the Beast Puppet and Mask Theatre of Minneapolis took for its theme "We Are Water." The giant animals and figures, handmade from newspaper, flour-and-water paste, and imagination, told the story of the seas and the creatures who live there, with a special Minnesota emphasis. A towering image of the "Mother of Waters" reminded Minnesotans of the state's 10,000-plus lakes and unique position as the point of origin of waters that flow to all the points of the compass.

Water brought the traders and explorers and settlers

who helped build Minnesota. The state's sky-blue waters will continue to be its greatest asset in the twenty-first century. Minnesotans must work to clean up and to prevent pollution of those waterways, just as they are now working to purify the air. The state belongs to each and every Minnesotan.

Held proudly aloft by puppeteers, this papier-mâché figure of "Mother of Waters" was designed by artist Anne Sawyer Aitch for In the Heart of the Beast Puppet and Mask Theatre's annual May Day Parade in Minneapolis in 2007.

ACTIVITIES

BAKING WITH BLUEBERRIES

July is blueberry time in Minnesota. Pick your own at a fruit farm or buy Minnesota-grown berries at the St. Paul Farmer's Market. Using the recipe below, bake blueberry muffins for breakfast. (Be sure to wait until an adult can help you in the kitchen.) You can freeze the berries you don't use. Just wash the excess berries well, blot them dry on a paper towel, spread them in a single layer on a cookie sheet, and put them in the freezer for one hour. Remove the frozen berries from the freezer, put them in a plastic freezer bag or container, and return them to the freezer. That way you can have a taste of summer in the fall, winter, and spring!

OFFICIAL MINNESOTA
BLUEBERRY MUFFIN RECIPE

1/2 cup softened butter

1 1/4 cups sugar

2 eggs

2 cups flour

1/2 teaspoon salt

2 teaspoons baking powder

1/2 cup milk

1 cup fresh Minnesota blueberries

1 teaspoon grated orange peel

3 teaspoons of sugar (for sprinkling)

Preheat oven to 375 degrees F. Cream together the butter and sugar. Add eggs one at a time, beating well after each addition. In a separate bowl sift together the flour, salt, and baking powder. Add the dry ingredients to the creamed mixture a little at a time, alternating with the milk. Crush half a cup of the blueberries with a fork and add to batter. Fold in half a cup of whole berries and the orange peel. Mix thoroughly, but batter should be slightly lumpy. Fill large muffin cups (use paper liners) with batter. Sprinkle tops with sugar. Bake 20 to 30 minutes and cool before removing from pan. *Makes 6 Minnesota muffins.*

WHAT'S IN A NAME?

Minnesota is nicknamed the Gopher State, but is there any difference between a gopher, a chipmunk, and a thirteen-striped ground squirrel? Using the Internet or library reference books, research each rodent. Prepare a written report (be sure to include photos) and share it with your classmates.

ACTIVITIES

chapter one

MINNESOTA (WO)MAN

Although the remains of Minnesota's earliest known resident are those of a girl, she was originally called "Minnesota Man." Some people objected to the mislabeling, however. They felt the label should be changed to be more accurate. Using the Internet or library reference books, research how the name of the Minnesota Man officially became Minnesota Woman.

MINNESOTA'S DAKOTA AND OJIBWE

Minnesota is home to eleven First Nations communities. Included among the seven Ojibwe communities is the Grand Portage Reservation, which relives its fur-trading heritage during Rendezvous Days in mid-August. Included among the four Dakota communities is the Prairie Island band of Mdewakanton Dakota. Using the Internet or library reference books, learn what life is like for Minnesota's Ojibwe and Dakota in the twenty-first century. How do they preserve and honor their heritage and culture?

Indian doll made of leather, feathers, and beads, ca. 2006.

chapter two

VISIT A LOCK AND DAM

The Mississippi River runs the length of Minnesota, from Lake Itasca in the north, through Lake Pepin near Red Wing, and down to La Crescent at the southern tip of the state. The U.S. Army Corps of Engineers operates twenty-nine locks and dams along the entire Mississippi. What is a lock and dam? How many locks and dams are on the river in Minnesota? Which Minnesota lock has the deepest drop? Visit the U.S. Army Corps of Engineers Web site (www.usace.army.mil) or visit one of the state's locks and dams to learn more about how this engineering marvel has created "steps" in the river that control traffic and water levels for barges and boats.

ACTIVITIES

chapter three

EARLY NEWSPAPERS

Back in James Goodhue's time, newspapers were printed by hand. Every letter of every word in every sentence of every paragraph was handset in metal type. How long would it have taken a typesetter to print an eight-page newspaper? How were pictures reproduced? How many papers would need to be sold to make a profit? Newspapers tell more than local and national stories, of course; they are a record of the things we buy. At the library or the Minnesota Historical Society, look at the ads in newspapers published fifty and one hundred years ago. What did items like a coat or a loaf of bread or a car (or a carriage!) cost in those early years of the state?

MAKE A MINNESOTA TIMELINE

With your classmates, make a Minnesota timeline for your classroom. Each student can prepare a section of the timeline. Use one sheet of 8½-by-11-inch construction paper for each decade of Minnesota's history.

chapter four

ABOLITION IN MINNESOTA

Minnesota went on record in 1854 that it would not tolerate slavery. But not everyone in the state believed African Americans deserved their freedom. Using the Internet or library reference books, learn how Minnesotans helped promote abolition in the years before and after the Civil War. Was Minnesota part of the Underground Railroad, a secret network of people who helped southern slaves find their way to freedom in the North?

INDIAN ADVOCATE

Henry Benjamin Whipple, Minnesota's first Episcopal bishop, was an advocate for the Indians of Minnesota for the last half of the nineteenth century. He asked several U.S. presidents, including Abraham Lincoln and Ulysses S. Grant, to help the state's Dakota and Ojibwe. Using the Internet or library reference books, research Bishop Whipple's important work on behalf of the Indians in Minnesota.

Bishop Henry Benjamin Whipple, ca. 1862.

ACTIVITIES

chapter five

MINNESOTA HALL OF FAME

Minnesota is home to many businesses and products of national and international fame, like 3M's Post-it Notes, Hormel's Spam, and Red Wing Shoes. Using the Internet and library reference books, list as many well-known businesses and products founded in Minnesota as you can. Don't forget Dairy Queen and Rollerblades and the snowmobile! Find or print pictures of the famous products. What is Minnesota's oldest invention or product or company still in existence?

THE LONG WINTER

Laura Ingalls Wilder grew up in Walnut Grove, Minnesota, during the 1870s. As an adult she wrote her *Little House on the Prairie* books. Read her sixth book in the series, *The Long Winter*. What happened during that winter of 1880–1881 to make it so severe? How did the Ingalls family survive? How did they pass the long hours indoors? What would you do if you were snowed in for weeks, without television, without an MP3 player, without electricity at all?

chapter six

MEDICAL MILESTONES

Minnesotans know about the Doctors Mayo, who founded the world-famous clinic, and about Medtronic, which created the world's first battery-powered heart pacemaker. But who remembers that woman from Australia who came to Minnesota to treat a dread childhood disease called polio? Using the Internet and library reference books, learn more about Sister Elizabeth Kenny and her therapies. Research other medical firsts in Minnesota, such as the first open-heart surgery at the University of Minnesota.

APPLE TASTE TEST

Once considered impossible for growing apples, Minnesota has had the last laugh. The state boasts more than twenty apple varieties, from Beacon to Honey Crisp to Viking. Harvest time starts the third week of July and lasts until the second week of October. Set up an apple taste test in your classroom and try as many varieties as you can to find the one you like best, especially dipped in caramel! And visit one of Minnesota's many apple orchards. There are more than forty in the Twin Cities area alone!

The Honeycrisp apple!

ACTIVITIES

chapter seven

MINNESOTA ARCHITECTURE

Cass Gilbert is perhaps the architect most often associated with Minnesota, but there are many other famous designers of business and residential structures in the state. Look at Twin Cities buildings on www.citiesarchitecture.com or similar Web sites. Take a tour of a neighborhood that is known for its architecture. What architectural styles were popular in each of Minnesota's decades of existence?

MINNESOTA GARDENS

The *Spoonbridge and Cherry* fountain at the Minneapolis Sculpture Garden. In summer, water flows over the surface of the cherry and a fine mist rises from its stem (see p. 130).

The Minneapolis Sculpture Garden of the Walker Art Center is one of the most popular of all Minnesota gardens. But other public gardens in the state have their own attractions. Visit the Eloise Butler Wildflower Garden, the nation's oldest wildflower garden, on Wirth Parkway in Minneapolis. Or take a tour of the Florence Bakken Physic Garden, which is filled with plants with healing powers, at the Bakken Museum of Electricity in Minneapolis. Or stroll within the Normandale Japanese Gardens of Bloomington, which is landscaped with oriental-style bridges, lanterns, and waterfalls.

chapter eight

VISIT A LIVING HISTORY MUSEUM

Dressed in costumes of the times, employees at living history museums show visitors how people lived and worked long ago. Take a field trip with your classmates to one of Minnesota's living history museums listed below.

Fort Snelling (St. Paul)

Oliver H. Kelley Museum (Elk River)

Gibbs Museum of Pioneer and Dakotah Life (St. Paul)

North West Company Fur Post (Pine City)

Grand Portage National Monument (Grand Portage)

Forest History Center (Grand Rapids)

Historic Forestville (Preston)

Village of Yesteryear (Owatonna)

ACTIVITIES

chapter nine

The historic Oliver H. Kelley farm near Elk River, Minnesota.

PLAN A PARTY!

Minnesota governor Tim Pawlenty appointed a Minnesota Sesquicentennial Commission in 2005. The commissioners have been responsible for creating a "plan for capital improvements, celebratory activities, and public engagement." It has also been their duty to raise the money needed to celebrate Minnesota's 150th birthday in every county in the state. With your classmates, form your own sesquicentennial committee. Decide how you will kick off the celebration. What will be the celebration's grand finale? What activities will you hold in between? Which events will be just for kids? What special products will you sell? How will you raise money to pay for the celebration?

LAKE COUNTRY

Known as the Gopher State and the North Star State, Minnesota is also called the Land of 10,000 Lakes. The state is home to many notable lakes, including Lake Pepin and Lake Superior. Minnesota is also the place where scow sailing and water-skiing were invented. Using the Internet or library reference books, learn more about the history of Lake Superior, Minnesota's biggest lake and international port; about Minnesota's inventors of water-skiing and scow sailing; and about Minnesota's Boundary Waters Canoe Area Wilderness.

MINNESOTA IN THE MOVIES

What does Josh Hartnett have in common with Judy Garland, Winona Ryder, and the Coen brothers? They're all Minnesotans who made their Hollywood dreams come true. Using the Internet or library reference books, see how many made-in-Minnesota feature films you can list. How many homegrown actors and directors can you name?

SELECTED BIBLIOGRAPHY

Aby, Anne J., ed. *The North Star State: A Minnesota History Reader*. St. Paul: Minnesota Historical Society Press, 2002.

Bessler, John D. *Legacy of Violence: Lynch Mobs and Executions in Minnesota*. Minneapolis: University of Minnesota Press, 2003.

Blashfield, Jean F. *Awesome Almanac: Minnesota*. Fontana, WI: B & B Publishing, 1993

Blegen, Theodore C. *Minnesota: A History of the State,* 2nd ed. Minneapolis: University of Minnesota Press, 1975.

Boehme, Sarah E., Christian F. Feest, and Patricia Condon Johnston. *Seth Eastman: A Portfolio of North American Indians*. Afton, MN: Afton Historical Society Press, 1995.

Breining, Greg. *Minnesota*. Revised 3rd ed. New York: Fodor's, 2006.

Busch, Jason T., Christopher Monkhouse, and Janet L. Whitmore. *Currents of Change: Art and Life Along the Mississippi River, 1850-1861*. Minneapolis: Minneapolis Institute of Arts, 2004.

Carley, Kenneth. *The Dakota War of 1862*. St. Paul: Minnesota Historical Society Press, 1976.

Carley, Kenneth. *Minnesota in the Civil War: An Illustrated History*. St. Paul: Minnesota Historical Society Press, 2000.

Chrislock, Carl H. *Watchdog of Loyalty: The Minnesota Commission of Public Safety During World War I*. St. Paul: Minnesota Historical Society Press, 1991.

Clark, Jr., Clifford E., ed. *Minnesota in a Century of Change*. St. Paul: Minnesota Historical Society Press, 1989.

Coen, Rena Neumann. *Painting and Sculpture in Minnesota, 1820-1914*. Minneapolis: University of Minnesota Press, 1976.

Densmore, Frances. *Chippewa Customs*. 1929.

Reprint ed., St. Paul: Minnesota Historical Society Press, 1979.

Dregni, Eric. *Minnesota Marvels*. Minneapolis: University of Minnesota Press, 2001.

Eastman, Mary Henderson. *Dahcotah; or, Life and Legends of the Sioux*. 1849. Reprint ed., Afton, MN: Afton Historical Society Press, 1995.

El-Hai, Jack. *Minnesota Collects*. St. Paul: Minnesota Historical Society Press, 1992.

El-Hai, Jack. *Lost Minnesota: Stories of Vanished Places*. Minneapolis: University of Minnesota Press, 2000.

Fedo, Michael. *The Lynchings in Duluth*. St. Paul: Minnesota Historical Society Press, 2000.

Fedo, Michael. *The Pocket Guide to Minnesota Place Names*. St. Paul: Minnesota Historical Society Press, 2002.

Flandrau, Grace. *Memoirs of Grace Flandrau*. Compiled by Georgia Ray. St. Paul: Knochaloe Beg Press, 2003.

Folwell, William Watts. *A History of Minnesota*. Revised ed., St. Paul: Minnesota Historical Society, 1956.

Forester, Jeff. *The Forest for the Trees*. St. Paul: Minnesota Historical Society Press, 2004.

Frazier, Ian. *Great Plains*. New York: Farrar, Straus and Giroux, 1989.

Friendly, Fred W. *Minnesota Rag*. New York: Vintage Books, 1982.

Gardner, Denis P. *Minnesota Treasures*. St. Paul: Minnesota Historical Society Press, 2004.

Gilman, Carolyn. *The Grand Portage Story*. St. Paul: Minnesota Historical Society Press, 1992.

Gilman, Rhoda R. *Northern Lights: The Story of Minnesota's Past*. St. Paul: Minnesota Historical Society Press, 1989.

Gilman, Rhoda R. *Henry Hastings Sibley: Divided Heart*. St. Paul: Minnesota Historical Society Press, 2004.

Gilman, Rhoda R., and June Drenning Holmquist, eds. *Selections from "Minnesota History."* St. Paul: Minnesota Historical Society Press, 1965.

Grenier, Tony. *The Minnesota Book of Days: An Almanac of State History*. St. Paul: Minnesota Historical Society Press, 2001.

Hage, Dave, and Paul Klauda. *No Retreat, No Surrender: Labor's War at Hormel*. New York: Morrow, 1989.

Johnston, Patricia Condon. *Eastman Johnson's Lake Superior Indians*. Afton, MN: Johnston Publishing, 1983.

Johnston, Patricia Condon. *Minnesota: Portrait of the Land and its People*. Helena, MT: American Geographic Publishing, 1987.

Jones, Evan. *Citadel in the Wilderness: The Story of Fort Snelling and the Northwest Frontier*. 1966. Reprint ed., Minneapolis: University of Minnesota Press, 2001.

Keenan, Jerry. *The Great Sioux Uprising*. Cambridge, MA: Da Capo Press, 2003.

Keillor, Garrison. *Lake Wobegon Summer 1956*. New York: Viking, 2001.

Keillor, Steven J. *Grand Excursion: Antebellum America Discovers the Upper Mississippi*. Afton, MN: Afton Historical Society Press, 2004.

Knute, Grace Lee. *The Voyageur*. 1931. Reprint ed., St. Paul: Minnesota Historical Society Press, 1987.

Koutsky, Kathryn, and Linda Koutsky. *Minnesota Vacation Days*. St. Paul: Minnesota Historical Society Press, 2006.

Larson, Don W. *Land of the Giants: A History of Minnesota Business*. Minneapolis: Dorn Books, 1979.

Lass, William E. *Minnesota: A Bicentennial History.* New York: Norton, 1977.

Leaf, Sue. *Potato City.* St. Paul: Borealis Books, 2004.

Longfellow, Henry Wadsworth. *The Song of Hiawatha.* 1855. Reprint ed., Boston: David R. Godine, 2004.

Lovelace, Maud Hart. *Early Candlelight.* 1929. Reprint ed., St. Paul: Minnesota Historical Society Press, 1992.

Lovelace, Maud Hart. *Betsy-Tacy.* 1940. Reprint ed., New York: HarperCollins, 1995.

Marling, Karal Ann. *The Colossus of Roads.* 1984. 2nd ed., Minneapolis: University of Minnesota Press, 2000.

Marling, Karal Ann. *Blue Ribbon: A Social and Pictorial History of the Minnesota State Fair.* St. Paul: Minnesota Historical Society Press, 1990.

Mason. Philip P., ed. *Schoolcraft's Expedition to Lake Itasca.* East Lansing: Michigan State University Press, 1993.

McDermid, Chris, ed. *Minnesota Almanac 2000: The Almanac of the Millennium.* 4th ed., Taylors Falls, MN: John L. Brekke and Sons, 1999.

Meier, Peg. *Bring Warm Clothes: Letters and Photos from Minnesota's Past.* Minneapolis: Neighbors Publishing, 1981.

Meier, Peg. *Coffee Made Her Insane.* Minneapolis: Neighbors Publishing, 1988.

Millet, Larry. *Sherlock Holmes and the Secret Alliance.* New York: Penguin, 2001. See also *Sherlock Holmes and the Red Demon* (2001) *Sherlock Holmes and the Rune Stone Mystery* (2000), et al.

Moe, Richard. *The Last Full Measure: The Life and Death of the First Minnesota Volunteers.* New York: Avon, 1993.

Mona, Dave, and Dave Jarzyna. *Twenty-Five Seasons: The First Quarter Century of the Minnesota Twins.* Minneapolis: Mona Publications, 1986.

Monjeau-Marz, Corinne L. *The Dakota Internment at Fort Snelling.* St. Paul: Prairie Smoke Press, 2005.

Moore, Willard B. *Circles of Tradition: Folk Arts in Minnesota.* St. Paul: Minnesota Historical Society Press, 1989.

Morris, Lucy Leavenworth Wilder, ed. *Old Rail Fence Corners: Frontier Tales Told By Minnesota Pioneers.*

St. Paul: Minnesota Historical Society Press, 1979.

Nielsen, Richard, and Scott F. Wolter. *The Kensington Runestone: Compelling New Evidence.* Minnesota: Lake Superior Agate Publishing, 2006.

Nord, Mary Ann. *The National Register of Historic Places in Minnesota: A Guide.* St. Paul: Minnesota Historical Society Press, 2003.

O'Connor, William Van, ed. *A History of the Arts in Minnesota.* Minneapolis: University of Minnesota Press, 1958.

Pennefeather, Shannon M., ed. *Mill City: A Visual History of the Minneapolis Mill District.* St. Paul: Minnesota Historical Society Press, 2003.

Pond, Samuel W. *Dakota Life in the Upper Midwest.* St. Paul: Minnesota Historical Society Press, 1986.

Powell, L.W. *The Land of Lakes; or, The New Northwest.* 1875. Reprint ed., Roseville, MN: Park Genealogical Books, 2005.

Radzilowski, John. *Minnesota.* Northampton, MA: Interlink Books, 2006.

Reiersgord, Thomas E. *The Kensington Runestone: Its Place in History.* St. Paul: Pogo Press, 2001.

Risjord, Norman K. *A Popular History of Minnesota.* St. Paul: Minnesota Historical Society Press, 2005.

Roethke, Leigh. *Minnesota's Capitol: A Centennial Story.* Afton, MN: Afton Historical Society Press, 2005.

Rubinstein, Sarah P. *Minnesota History Along the Highways.* St. Paul: Minnesota Historical Society Press, 2003.

Schaper, Julie, and Steven Horwitz, eds. *Twin Cities Noir.* New York: Akashic Books, 2006.

Schultz, Duane. *Over the Earth I Come.* Leicester, England: F.A. Thorpe, 1993.

Shaw, Janet. *Meet Kirsten: An American Girl.* Middleton, WI: Pleasant Co., 1986.

Spencer, Tom. *Black Thursday: The Tracy Tornado, June 13, 1968.* Marshall, MN: Southwest History Center, 1993.

Stuhler, Barbara, and Gretchen Kreuter, eds. *Women of Minnesota.* Revised ed., St. Paul: Minnesota Historical Society Press, 1998.

Swanson, William. *Dial M: The Murder of Carol*

Thompson. St. Paul: Borealis Books, 2006.

Tice, D.J. *Minnesota's Twentieth Century.* Minneapolis: University of Minnesota Press, 1999.

Werle, Steve. *An American Gothic: The Life and Times and Legacy of William Gates LeDuc.* South Saint Paul: Dakota County Historical Society, 2004.

White, Helen M. *Henry Sibley's First Years at St. Peters or Mendota.* St. Paul: Turnstone Historical Research, 2002.

Wills, Jocelyn. *Boosters, Hustlers, and Speculators: Entrepreneurial Culture and the Rise of Minneapolis and St. Paul.* St. Paul: Minnesota Historical Society Press, 2005.

Wingerd, Mary Lethert. *Claiming the City: Politics, Faith, and the Power of Place in St. Paul.* Ithaca: Cornell University Press, 2001.

Winnan, Audur H. *Wanda Gág.* Washington, D.C.: Smithsonian Institution Press, 1993.

Works Progress Administration. *The WPA Guide to Minnesota.* 1938. Reprint ed., St. Paul: Minnesota Historical Society Press, 1985.

Federal Writers' Program of the Works Projects Administration. *The Bohemian Flats.* 1941. Reprint ed., St. Paul: Minnesota Historical Society Press, 1986.

Younger, Cole. *The Story of Cole Younger by Himself.* St. Paul: Minnesota Historical Society Press, 2000.

This list consists mainly of works I have enjoyed reading—and books that are easy to find in most public libraries and many bookstores. Any serious research on Minnesota history must begin in the holdings of the Minnesota Historical Society (MHS), however. Records and guides to using them can be found at www.mnhs.org. Another excellent source of information and interpretation is the Society's quarterly journal, *Minnesota History*. Special issues of *Minnesota History*, such as volume 56, number 4 (Winter 1998-99), "Making Minnesota Territory, 1849-1858," and volume 56, number 8 (Winter 1999-2000), "Minnesota Century," are especially useful. As this bibliography shows, the MHS continues to publish a remarkable torrent of excellent scholarship on Minnesota's past.

Finally, Minnesota is blessed with a vigorous local history movement, including county and municipal historical museums, state park guides, preservation societies, and interested laypersons. Everybody in Minnesota owns a share of our common history; join and support grassroots efforts to understand and to learn from our heritage.

ILLUSTRATION CREDITS

AFTON PRESS,
Afton, Minnesota
p. 48, sculpture of Hiawatha and Minnehaha, photographer Chuck Johnston.

HAZEL BELVO,
Minneapolis, Minnesota
p. 161, *Spirit Tree: Dusk I,* artist Hazel Belvo, Oil on Canvas 48" x 72", 1998-9.

KEIR BRISCO,
Oak Park, Illinois
p. 141, statue of Mary Tyler Moore, photographer Keir Brisco.

GAYLA ELLIS,
Minneapolis, Minnesota
p. 151, *Mother of Waters,* photographer Gayla Ellis.

GENERAL MILLS ARCHIVES,
Minneapolis, Minnesota
p. 134 (top), Betty Crocker spoon logo.

GRAND CASINO MILLE LACS,
Onamia, Minnesota
p. 63, Grand Casino and Hotel.

GRAHAM GREGORICH,
Columbia Heights, Minnesota
p. 149, Wednesday Bay of Crooked Lake, photographer Graham Gregorich, 2005.

GARY HARM and
UNIVERSITY OF MINNESOTA LIBRARIES,
Minneapolis, Minnesota
p. 125, sketch from *Millions of Cats,* artist Wanda Gág.

LIBRARY OF CONGRESS,
Washington, D.C.
p. 32, "Song catcher" Frances Densmore.

W. D. MACMILLAN FAMILY and
AFTON HISTORICAL SOCIETY PRESS,
Afton, Minnesota
p. 28, *Dacotah Village,* artist Seth Eastman; **p. 35,** *The Laughing Waters,* artist Seth Eastman, ca. 1850; **p. 36,** *Falls of St. Anthony,* artist Seth Eastman; **p. 45,** *Henry Schoolcraft at Lake Itasca,* artist Seth Eastman.

MALL OF AMERICA,
Bloomington, Minnesota
p. 139 (right), north entrance.

KARAL ANN MARLING,

Minneapolis, Minnesota
p. 9, seed portrait, artist Lillian Colton; **p. 59** (top), collectible plate.

MINNEAPOLIS CLUB,
Minneapolis, Minnesota
p. 89, Dalrymple Farm, engraving by Berghary.

MINNEAPOLIS INSTITUTE OF ARTS,
Minneapolis, Minnesota
p. 42, E. Jaccard and Company silver pitcher; **p. 101** (bottom), presentation tray; **p. 115,** *Rainy Evening on Hennepin Avenue,* artist Robert Koehler, ca. 1910.

MINNEAPOLIS PUBLIC LIBRARY,
Minneapolis, Minnesota
p. 104, Exposition Building, 1893; **p. 105,** Old Minneapolis City Hall, 1886; **p. 122** (left), Rand Tower.

MINNESOTA HISTORICAL SOCIETY,
St. Paul, Minnesota
p. 2, Moccasin flower, postcard; **p. 12,** Greetings from Minnesota, postcard ca. 1960; **p. 15,** State Seal, 1949; **p. 16** (top), "Willie Walleye" statue, photographer Guenin Photo Studio, postcard ca. 1960; **p. 19** (top), The Minnesota Centennial Train, poster, 1958; **p. 19** (bottom), young boy, August, 1958; **p. 20,** centennial emblem trivet, 1958; **p. 21,** *Great Northern Diver or Loon,* artist John James Audubon, 1836; **p. 22** (bottom), gopher train, artist R. O. Sweeny; **p. 23,** legislators, photographer *St. Paul Dispatch & Pioneer Press,* 1931; **p. 26,** petroglyphs, photographer Alan Ominsky, 1967; **p. 27** (left), Kensington runestone, ca. 1920; **p. 29,** illustration by Carl W. Bertsch from *The Voyageur* by Grace Lee Nute, (Minnesota Historical Society Press, 1931); **p. 34,** Joe Rolette, artist unknown, pastel, ca. 1900; **p. 38** (top), Colonel Josiah Snelling, ca. 1820; **p. 38** (bottom), Lawrence Taliaferro, artist unknown, oil, ca. 1830; **p. 39,** Fort Snelling, artist Edward K. Thomas (1817-1906), oil, ca. 1850; **p. 40** (top), Henry Hastings Sibley, artist Thomas Cantwell Healy, oil, 1860; **p. 40** (bottom), Henry Sibley's dog Lion, artist Charles Deas, 1841; **p. 41,** *Father Hennepin at the Falls of St. Anthony,* artist Douglas Volk, ca. 1905; **p. 43,** Henry Rowe Schoolcraft, ca. 1855; **p. 46** (bottom), Pipestone Quarry, photographer William Henry Illingworth, stereograph ca. 1880; **p. 47** (bottom), scene from Minnehaha and Hiawatha, photographer Keystone View Company, stereograph ca. 1900; **p. 49,** *Fort Snelling 1848, Head of Navigation* by Seth Eastman; **p. 50,** Red River cart train, photographer James E. Martin, ca. 1858-1859; **p. 52,** buckskin coat, museum collections; **p. 53** (top), Alexander Ramsey and Alexander Jenks Ramsey, ca. 1849; **p. 53** (bottom), Sibley House, artist J. H. Armstrong, watercolor, ca. 1888;

p. 54, *Treaty of Traverse des Sioux,* artist Frank Blackwell Mayer, ca. 1905; **p. 56,** printing press, ca. 1836; **p. 57** (top), William Gates LeDuc, ca. 1848; **p. 57** (bottom), Pioneer & Democrat Office, watercolor, 1858; **p. 58,** Main Avenue of the New York Crystal Palace, *The Art Journal,* 1851; **p. 59** (bottom), state capitol, photographer Whitney's Gallery, carte-de-visite, ca. 1865; **p. 60,** emigration poster, 1857; **p. 61** (left), Ignatius Donnelly, photographer Matthew Brady, ca. 1865; **p. 62** (top), Jane Grey Swisshelm, photographer Eugene S. Hill (1856-1936), cabinet photograph, 1852; **p. 62** (bottom), home of Jane Grey Swisshelm, ambrotype, ca. 1858; **p. 64,** *Battle of Nashville,* artist Howard Pyle, 1906; **p. 66,** First Minnesota Volunteers, postcard, 1861; **p 67,** Willis A. Gorman, photographer Whitney's Gallery, ca. 1862; **p. 68,** Knute Nelson, ambrotype, ca. 1862; **p. 69** (left), Archbishop John Ireland, photographer A. Larson, 1862; **p. 69** (right), Samuel D. Badger, artist unknown, pastel, ca. 1870; **p. 70,** commemorative postcard, ca. 1910; **p. 71,** Brigadier General William Gates LeDuc, 1863; **p. 73,** 1862 Acton attack, sketch, 1909; **p. 74,** Carrothers children, tintype, ca. 1872; **p. 75** (top), Henry H. Sibley, ca. 1865; **p. 75** (bottom), people escaping from the Indian massacre of 1862, photographer Adrian J. Ebell, carte-de-visite, August 21, 1862; **p. 76,** *Attack on New Ulm 1862,* artist Anton Gág, oil, 1904; **p. 77,** *The Attack at New Ulm,* Art Collection, wood engraving; **p. 78** (top), confirmation, photographer Benjamin Franklin Upton, carte-de-visite, April 1863; **p. 78** (bottom), bounty check; **p. 79** (left), *Cha-tan-wah-ka-wah-ma-nee,* artist Frank Blackwell Mayer, oil, 1895; **p. 79** (right), Grand Army of the Republic medal; **p. 81,** 28th Virginia Infantry battle flag, artist John A. Weide, oil, 1895; **p. 82,** wheat farm, artist James R. Meeker, 1877; **p. 83,** wagonload of wheat, ca. 1900; **p. 84** (top), steam engine, ca. 1910; **p. 84** (bottom), harvesting wheat, postcard, ca. 1986; **p. 85,** Paul Bunyan, postcard, ca. 1938; **p. 86** (left), advertising booklet, 1914; **p. 86** (right), chainsaw; **p. 87,** lumberjack camp, ca. 1885; **p. 90,** The *William Crooks,* photographer Moses C. Tuttle, 1864; **p. 91** (top), James J. Hill, artist Adolf Muller-Ury, oil, ca. 1890; **p. 91** (bottom), James J. Hill House, ca. 1891; **p. 93** (top), Washburn A Mill, photographer William H. Jacoby, ca. 1875; **p. 93** (bottom), Washburn A Mill, ca. 1875; **p. 94,** open pit mine at Biwabik, 1895; **p. 95,** Tower-Soudan mine, 1890; **p. 96,** The grasshopper plague, engraving, 1888; **p. 97,** Stone Arch Bridge, postcard, ca. 1905; **p. 98,** parade float, 1893; **p. 100,** grocer's arch, 1883; **p. 101** (top), arch, 1883; **p. 102,** State Fair midway, 1895; **p. 103,** Horticulture Building, state fairgrounds, postcard, ca. 1905; **p. 106,** St. Paul Winter Carnival, chromolithograph, 1889; **p. 108** (top), Minnesota State Building, 1893; **p. 108** (bottom), display of Minnesota agriculture, 1904; **p. 109,** silver

Right: Minnesota's centuries-old *Spirit Tree* at Grand Portage by artist Hazel Belvo.

punchbowl; **p. 110**, butter dress; **p. 111** (top), the Doctors Mayo, ca. 1900; **p. 111** (bottom), William W. Mayo house, artist Jo Lutz Rollins, watercolor, 1942; **p. 112**, State Capitol building, postcard, ca. 1907; **p. 113**, ground breaking, 1896; **p. 114** (top), mural, 1905; **p. 114** (bottom), The *Quadriga*, 1949; **p. 116** (top), Thomas B. Walker's art gallery, ca. 1890; **p. 116** (bottom), *St. Paul from Dayton's Bluff*, artist Alexis Fournier, 1888; **p. 117**, Minneapolis Institute of Arts, postcard, ca. 1920; **p. 118**, Sinclair Lewis home, postcard, ca. 1970; **p. 119** (left), Grace Flandrau, ca. 1920; **p. 119** (right), F. Scott Fitzgerald, Kregel Photo Parlors, ca. 1917; **p. 120** (left), Minneapolis City Hall, 1903; **p. 120** (right), Cathedral of St. Paul, architect E. Masqueray, 1908; **p. 121** (left), St. Paul City and County Building, artist Ferdinand Uebel, watercolor, 1937; **p. 121** (right), working man's house, ca. 1910; **p. 122** (right), Peavy-Haglin grain elevator, 1908; **p. 123** (top), Brainerd opera house, ca. 1905; **p. 123** (bottom), St. Paul's Grand Opera House, ca. 1870; **p. 124**, Metropolitan Opera House, ca. 1910; **p. 126**, Corn and Potato Palace, postcard, 1907; **p. 127** (left), Miss Minne Sota, postcard, 1907; **p. 127** (right), *Christmas Eve on the Flats*, artist Samuel Chatwood Burton, oil, 1919; **p. 128** (top), *Frances Cranmer Greenman*, artist Dewey Albinson, ca. 1925; **p. 128** (bottom), Dewey Albinson and Leonard Hendrickson, photograph, 1922; **p. 131**, Charles A. Lindbergh Jr., ca. 1927; **p. 132**, Northwest Airlines plane, ca. 1950; **p. 133**, fan board, 1991; **p. 134** (bottom), Dr. Norman Ernest Borlaug, ca. 1970; **p. 135**, turkey barn, ca. 1947; **p. 136** (top), Governor Wendell Anderson, 1974; **p. 136** (bottom), log cabins, postcard, ca. 1940; **p. 137**, Foshay Tower, photographer Norton & Peel, 1931; **p. 139** (left), Vikings fans, photographer John Doman, 1981; **p. 140** (bottom), Guthrie Theatre, photographer Terry Garvey, 1966; **p. 142** (top), Walter Mondale and Hubert H. Humphrey, 1975; **p. 142** (bottom), Eugene McCarthy and Michael McCarthy, photographer Perrone Incorporated, 1958; **p. 144** (top), Frank B. Kellogg, artist C. B. Pereira, oil, ca. 1930; **p. 145** (top), Clelland Card, ca. 1940; **p. 145** (bottom), Hubert H. Humphrey, photographer *Minneapolis Tribune*, 1946; **p. 157**, Kelley farm; **p. 164**, *Countryside of Minnesota*, artist Adolf Dehn, watercolor, 1960.

MINNESOTA LANDSCAPE ARBORETUM,
Chaska, Minnesota
p. 155, Honeycrisp apple.

MINNESOTA VIKINGS,
Eden Prairie, MN
p. 143, Vikings football team, 1969.

MISSOURI HISTORICAL SOCIETY
MUSEUM COLLECTIONS, St. Louis, Missouri
p. 61 (right), portrait of Dred Scott, oil on canvas by Louis Schultze, 1888. Acc. # 1897.9.1. Photograph by David Schultz, 1999. Photograph and scan © 1997-2006, Missouri Historical Society.

NATIONAL MISSISSIPPI RIVER MUSEUM &
AQUARIUM, CAPTAIN WILLIAM D. BOWELL, SR.,
RIVER LIBRARY,
Dubuque, Iowa
p. 44, Giacomo Beltrami, by artist Ken Fox.

DANA NYE,
Los Angeles, California
p. 140 (top), Prairie Home Companion Radio Show.

BENJAMIN OEHLER,
Wayzata, Minnesota
p. 154, Bishop Henry Benjamin Whipple.

OFFICE OF THE MINNESOTA
SECRETARY OF STATE,
St. Paul, Minnesota
p. 14, state seal; **p. 17**, *Grace*, photographer Eric Enstrom, 1918.

OTTER TAIL COUNTY HISTORICAL SOCIETY,
Fergus Falls, Minnesota
p. 25, Minnesota Woman monument, photographer LeAnn Neuleib, 2007.

PENUMBRA THEATRE COMPANY,
St. Paul, Minnesota
p. 129 (top), Quilt Wall, artist Chad Van Kekerix, photographer Ann Marsden; **p. 129** (bottom), Lou Bellamy, photographer Ann Marsden.

BRUCE PETTIT,
Afton, Minnesota
p. 27 (right), Big Ole.

PRIVATE COLLECTION
p. 8, *Fort Snelling*, artist Paul Kramer, oil on canvas, 1992; **p. 153**, doll.

PRIVATE COLLECTION
p. 31, *The Canoe Builders of Saganaga*, artist Howard Sivertson, oil on canvas.

ST. LOUIS COUNTY HISTORICAL SOCIETY,
Duluth, Minnesota
p. 24, *Canoe of Indians*, artist Eastman Johnson; **p. 33**, *Camp Scene at Grand Portage*, artist Eastman Johnson, 1857.

SCIENCE MUSEUM OF MINNESOTA,
St. Paul, Minnesota
p. 146, Science Museum, photographer Eric Mueller.

HOWARD SIVERTSON,
Grand Marais, Minnesota
p. 30, *The Annual Cycle*.

SMITHSONIAN AMERICAN ART MUSEUM,
Washington, DC / Art Resource, New York
p. 46 (top), Blue Medicine, artist George Catlin, 1835.

STILLWATER PUBLIC LIBRARY,
Stillwater, Minnesota
p. 80, Civil War veterans, photographer John Runk, ca. 1920, St. Croix Collection.

UNITED STATES POST OFFICE,
Washington, D.C.
p. 47 (top), Henry Wadsworth Longfellow Stamp Design © 2007 United States Postal Service. All Rights Reserved. Used with Permission.

UNIVERSITY OF MINNESOTA - TC,
Minneapolis, Minnesota
p. 22 (top), Goldy Gopher.

WALKER ART CENTER,
Minneapolis, Minnesota
p. 130, *Spoonbridge and Cherry*, sculptors Claes Oldenburg and Coosje van Bruggen.

WCCO TV,
Minneapolis, Minnesota
p. 11, Don Shelby.

WIKIMEDIA COMMONS,
en.wikipedia.org
p. 4, Landmark Center; **p. 138**, IDS Center; **p. 156**, *Spoonbridge and Cherry*.

ASHLEY WILKES, University of Minnesota,
Minneapolis, Minnesota
p. 16 (bottom), nail file; **p. 152**, blueberry muffin.

INDEX

African Americans, 35, 81, 143, 148, 150
    and Penumbra Theater, 128-129, **129**
Albinson, Dewey, 128
    and Greenman, Frances Cranmer, **128**
Anderson, Wendell, 135-136, **136,** 140
Apples, 17-18, 107
    and Honeycrisp, 149, **155**
Audubon, John James
    and *Great Northern Diver or Loon*, **21**

Badger, Samuel D., **69**
Basilica of St. Mary, 126, 130
Bellamy, Lou, 128-129, **129**
Beltrami, Giacomo, **44,** 44
Blackmun, Harry, 141
Blueberry muffin, 14, **152**
Bohemian Flats, 127-128
    and *Christmas Eve on the Flats*
        by S. Chatwood Burton, **127**
Bonaparte, Napoleon, 37
Boundary Waters Canoe Area, 137, 148-149, **149**
Brainerd
    and opera house, **123**
Brooks, Herb, 142
Browns Valley Man, 25
Buffington, Leroy, 121-122
Burger, Warren, 141

Cass, Lewis, 38, 43-44
Cathedral of St. Paul, 120, **120**
Catlin, George, 46
    and *Blue Medicine*, **46**
Civil War, 39, 61, 66, 72, 74, 83, 135
    and First Minnesota Infantry, **64, 66**, 68-70,
    and Grand Army of the Republic, 79-81
    and 28th Virginia Infantry battle flag, 81, **81**
Clark, William, 37, 51

Dalrymple, Oliver, **89,** 89, 92
Dayton's, 134, 138
Dehn, Adolf
    and *Countryside of Minnesota*, **164**
Densmore, Frances, **32,** 32, 117
Donnelly, Ignatius, 59-60, **61,** 66
Duluth, 94, 110
    and Congdon, Elizabeth, 143
    and *Edmund Fitzgerald*, 142
    and Metropolitan Opera House, **124**
    and railroads, 46, 91

Eastman, Mary, 13, 48-49, 112
Eastman, Seth, 13, 28, 35-36, 45, 48, 117
    and *Dacotah Village*, **28**
    and *Falls of St. Anthony*, **36**
    and Fort Snelling, **49,** 49
    and *Henry Schoolcraft at Lake Itasca*, **45**
    and *The Laughing Waters*, **35**
Ely
    and Boundary Waters Canoe Area, 137
    and *Burley's Cabins*, **136**
    and Steger, Will, 137
Enstrom, Eric, 14
    and *Grace*, 16-17, **17**

Falls of St. Anthony, 17, **36**, 39, 45, 65, 104,
    and flour-milling, 14, 83, 88
    and Hennepin, Father Louis, 40-41, **41**, 110
    and lumber-milling, 85,
    and Stone Arch Bridge, 97
    and tourism, 42-43, 48, 135
Faribault, Alexander, 33
First Minnesota Infantry, 67-71, 79
    and Last Man's Club, **80**
First Minnesota Regiment, 66-67. *Also see*
    First Minnesota Infantry
Fitzgerald, F. Scott, 118, **119**
Flandrau, Grace, **119,** 119
Flour, 14, 39, 58, 61, 83
    and railroads, 88-90
    and Stone Arch Bridge, 97
    and Washburn "A" Mill Explosion, **93,** 93
Fort Snelling, **8, 39**, 42, 48, 74, 107, 136, 143
    and Beltrami, Giacomo, 44
    and Civil War, 66-68
    and Eastman, Seth and Mary, 49, **49**
    and establishment of, 33, 38-40
    and Scott, Dred, 61
    and Taylor, Zachary, 52
    and U.S.-Dakota War of 1862, 71-72, 76-78
Fort St. Anthony
    See Fort Snelling
Foshay Tower, 137, **137**
Fournier, Alexis, 115-116
    and *St. Paul from Dayton's Bluff*, **116**
Fur trade, 29-33, 37, 58

Gág, Anton, 115
    Attack on New Ulm 1862, **76**
Gág, Wanda, 124
    Millions of Cats, **125**
General Mills, 134, 145
    Betty Crocker, **134**
Gettysburg
    and First Minnesota Volunteers, 68, **70,** 70, 81
Gilbert, Cass, 112-113
Goodhue, James, 55, 71
    and *Minnesota Pioneer*, **56,** 56
Gophers, **22,** 22-23,
Gorman, Willis, 58, **67,** 67-68
Grand Army of the Republic, 70, 79-80, **79**
Grand Casino Mille Lacs, **63**
Grand Excursion of 1854, 42
    and E. Jaccard and Company silver pitcher, **42**
Grand Portage, 24, 29-33, **33**
Grasshopper Plague of 1877, **96,** 96-97
Great Sioux Uprising. *See*
    U.S.-Dakota War of 1862
Greely, Horace, 18, 55-57
Greenman, Frances Cranmer, **128**
Guerin, Vital, 33
Guthrie Theater, 129, 139-140, **140,** 148

Hamsun, Knute, 92
Hennepin, Father Louis, 40-41, **41**, 110
Hill, James J., **91,** 125
    and art, 116-117
    and Great Northern Railroad, 89-92, 98, **98,** 109, **109**
    and James J. Hill House, **91**

and Minneapolis, 101
    and Stone Arch Bridge, 97, **101**
Hmong, 133, 143, 150
Homestead Act, 80, 86
Hormel, 134
Humphrey, Hubert, 141, **142, 145**

IDS Tower, 137-138, **138**
In the Heart of the Beast Puppet and Mask Theatre, **151**
Indian. *See*
    Native American
Ireland, John, 68-69, **69**
Iron Range, 44, 93-94, **94, 95**, 107, 109, 144
Isolationism, 132-133
Itasca, Lake, 44

Jeffers Petroglyphs, **26**
Jefferson, Thomas, 37
Johnson, Eastman, 33
    and *Camp Scene at Grand Portage*, **33**
    and *Canoe of Indians*, **24**

Keillor, Garrison
    and *Prairie Home Companion*, **140,** 140
Kellogg, Frank B., **144,** 144
Kensington Runestone, 26-27, **27**
    and Big Ole, **27**
King, Bill, 103-104
Koehler, Robert, 115
    and *Rainy Evening on Hennepin Avenue*, **115**
Korean War, 133

Lady's slipper, **2,** 14, **16**
Latinos, 143, 145, 150
Leavenworth, Henry, 38
LeDuc, William Gates, 56-58, **57**, 70-71, **71**
Lewis, Meriwether, 37, 51
Lewis, Sinclair, **118,** 118
Lincoln, Abraham, 62, 66, 75, 77
Lindbergh, Charles A. Jr., 131-132, **132**
Little Crow, 72-74, 78-79, **79**
    and bounty check, **78**
Long, Stephen, 34, 37, 44
Longfellow, Henry Wadsworth, **47**
    and *Song of Hiawatha*, 35, 43, **47,** 47-48
Louisiana Territory, 37
Lovelace, Maud Hart, 39-40, 110
Lumber, 85-86
    and logging, **86, 87**
    and Paul Bunyan, **85, 86**

Mall of America, 138-139, **139**, 148
Manifest Destiny, 18, 19, 51, 55
Marling, Karal Ann, **9**
Mayo, William Worrall, 77, **111,** 111
McCarthy, Eugene, 141, **142**
Meeker, James R., **82**
Mendota Treaty, 55, 72
Millett, Larry, 125-126
Minneapolis, 39, 42
    and Aquatennial, 99, 107, 143
    and architecture, 121
    and competition with St. Paul, 101-110
    and downtown development, 137

and flour-milling, 58, 88-89, 93
and Milwaukee Avenue, 121, *121*
and Minneapolis Exposition, *104,* 104-106, 116-117
and railroads, 99-100
and Stone Arch Bridge, *97,* 97
and suspension bridge, 58, *59*
and Washburn, C.C., 85
Minneapolis City Hall, *105, 120,* 120, 137
Minneapolis Institute of Arts, *117,* 117
Minnehaha Falls, 43, 48
Minnesota Centennial, 18-20, *19, 20*
Minnesota Man, 25
and Minnesota Woman, *25*
Minnesota Mining and Manufacturing, 133
and Post-it Notes, *133*
Minnesota River, 17, 33, 37, 42, 54-55
Minnesota state anthem, *23,* 23
Minnesota State Fair, 81, *102, 103,* 110, 123, 125, 143, 145
and competition between Minneapolis and
St. Paul, 102-105
and Fitzgerald, F. Scott, 118, *119*
and Princess Kay of the Milky Way, *110*
Minnesota Twins, 142
Minnesota Vikings, *139,* 139, 142-143, *143*
Mississippi River, 13, 40-42
and Bohemian Flats, 127
and flooding, 99
and flour-milling, 14, 83
and Fort Snelling, 33
and headwaters, 43-45
and St. Paul Winter Carnival, 106
and settlem ent, 37-39
and Stone Arch Bridge, 97
Mondale, Walter, 141, *142*
Moore, Mary Tyler, *141*
Moua, Mee, 150-151

Native Americans, *24,* 29, *31,* 31-33, *33,* 39-40, 43,
51, 53, 71, 117, 148, 150
and Blue Medicine, *46*
and Catlin, George, 46
and Dakota, 13, 18, 28, 32, 35, 37, 40, 48-49, 54-
55, 61, 66, 71-74, 76-79, 83, 143
and Eastman, Seth and Mary, 49
and First Nations, 25, 28
and Indian doll, *153*
and Longfellow, Henry Wadsworth, 47
and Ojibwe, 18, 28, 32, 35, 37, 41, 44, 55, 61, 68, 85,
143
and Swisshelm, Jane Grey, 62
and treaty rights, 63
and Treaty of Traverse des Sioux, *54,* 54-56
and U.S.-Dakota War of 1862, 72-78
Nelson, Knute, *68,* 107
New Ulm
and U.S.-Dakota War of 1862, 75
Nininger, John. *See*
Nininger, Minnesota
Nininger, Minnesota, 59-60, *60*
Northwest Airlines, 132, *132*
Northwest Ordinance of 1787, 33
Nute, Grace Lee, 29, 31
and *The Voyageur,* *29*

Oliver H. Kelley Farm, *84,* *157*

Panic of 1857, 59
Peavey-Haglin grain elevator, *122,* 122
Pike, Zebulon, 37

Pioneer & Democrat, *57*
Pipestone Quarry, *46*
Pond, Samuel, 32, 48
Postcards, *12,* 124-126
and Anoka Corn and Potato Palace, *126*
and "Miss Minne Sota", *127*

Railroads, 23, 90-91, 99, 144
and Grand Excursion of 1854, 42
and Great Northern, 89, 91, 97-98, 109
and Northern Pacific, 89, 99, 101
and transcontinental line, 83
and wheat, 88-89
Ramsey, Alexander, *53,* 59, 148
and appointment to territorial governorship, 52-53
and buckskin coat, *52*
and Civil War, 66-68
and U.S.-Dakota War of 1862, 75, 77
Rand Tower, *122*
Red River Valley, 34, *50,* 50-51, 88
Renville, Joseph, 34
Republican National Convention, 104-105
Revolutionary War, 25, 33
Rogers, Prince Nelson, 141
Rolette, Joe, *34,* 34,
Rolvaag, O.E., 92, 118
Rondeau, Joseph, 33

St. Anthony
See Minneapolis
St. Cloud Visiter
See Swisshelm, Jane Grey
St. Paul, 33-34, 42-43, 50-53, 98
and boomtown, 57-58
and competition with Minneapolis, 101-110
and Grand Opera House, *123*
and Landmark Center, *4,* 138
and railroads, 46, 89, 99-100,
and State Capitol, *16, 59, 112, 113,* 113, *114*
and twentieth century development, 137-138
and Winter Carnival, 99, *106,* 106-107, 118, 143
St. Paul City and County Building, *121*
Schoolcraft, Henry Rowe, 38, *43,* 43-44, 117, 148
and discovery of Mississippi headwater, 45, *45*
and Eastman, Seth, 49
and Longfellow, Henry Wadsworth, 48
Science Museum of Minnesota, *146*
Scott, Dred, *61,* 61,
Shelby, Don, *11*
Sibley, Henry, 39-40, *40,* 53, 85, 148
and Lion, *40*
and Sibley House, *53*
and state seal, 13
and Treaty of Traverse des Sioux, 54
and U.S. Congress, 52, 60
and U.S.-Dakota War of 1862, 75-76, *75*
Slavery, 61-62, 65-67
Snelling, Josiah, *38,* 38, 143
Somalis, 133, 143, 150
Song of Hiawatha. See
Longfellow, Henry Wadsworth
Southdale, 138
Spam
See Hormel
Spiess, Gerry, 142
State Capitol, 59, 107, 125, 143
and art housed in, 41, 54, 114
and construction of, 113-114, 117,
State Seal, 13-14, *14, 15, 16*

Steger, Will, 137
Stillwater Convention, 52
Stone Arch Bridge, 97, 99, 101-102
Superior, Lake, 94, 142
and Cooke, Jay, 91
and fur trade, 29-30, 32
Swisshelm, Jane Grey, 62, *62,* 65, 75

Taliaferro, Lawrence, *38,* 38, 61
Taylor, Zachary, 52
Treaty of Traverse des Sioux, *54,* 54-55, 72
Turkeys, 134, *135*
Turner, Frederick Jackson, 131

Union Army, 66, 68, 71-72, 81
University of Minnesota, 19, 57, 104, 127-128
and anthem, 23
and Borlaug, Norman, *134,* 134
and Buffington, Leroy, 121
and Goldy Gopher, *22*
and Keillor, Garrison, 140
and Mayo, W.W., 111
U.S. Congress, 33, 51, 53, 60, 72
U.S.-Dakota War of 1862, 55, 73-79, *75,* 115
and Acton Attack, 72, *73*
and attack on New Ulm, 75, *76, 77*
and Carrothers children, *74*

Veblen, Thorstein, 119
Ventura, Jesse, 81, 109
Vietnam War, 142, 150
Vietnamese, 143
Villard, Henry
and completion of Northern Pacific Railroad, 99-100,
100, 101
Voyageurs, 13, 27, 51, 110
and fur trade, 29, 32-33
and Nute, Grace Lee, *29,* 31

Walker Art Center, 117, 148
and *Spoonbridge and Cherry,* *130, 156*
Walker, Thomas B., *116,* 116-117
War of 1812, 33, 37
Washburn, C.C., 85, 88, 93
Washington, D.C., 32, 52, 66, 73, 75
Washington, George, 37, 51, 53
WCCO Radio, 145
and Clelland Card, *145*
Wetterling, Patty, 142
Wheat, *83,* 83-84, *84*
and railroads, 89-91
Whipple, Henry Benjamin, 65, 96, *154*
and U.S.-Dakota War, 76, *78*
Wild rice, 14, 29, 57
William Crooks, 89-90, *90,* 100, *101*
Willie Walleye, *16*
Winston, Eliza, 65
World's Fair
and Chicago, 14, 48, 107-109, *108,* 113, 125, 131
and New York 26, 56, *58*
and St. Louis, *108,* 109-110
World War I, 132
World War II, 16, 133

Youngdahl, Luther, 26

This book was designed with care by

Mary Susan Oleson
NASHVILLE, TENNESSEE